One Man's Wilderness

AN ALASKAN ODYSSEY

By Sam Keith from the journals and photographs of Richard Proenneke

Praise for *One Man's Wilderness:*

"Richard Proenneke, an emigre from Iowa to Alaska, kept a journal during the time he was fulfilling his dream of living in an altogether undeveloped part of Alaska. Parts of that journal have been made into a book by Sam Keith, along with colored photos that prove Alaska is certainly one of, if not the, most beautiful places anywhere."

—*Boston Globe*

"*One Man's Wilderness* is the best modern piece of prose about Alaska, the one that gives the truest picture of what living in the bush today is like for the lone individual."

—*Anchorage Daily News*

"Proenneke answered Robert Service's call of the wild. His journal forms the text of this handsome book, and his sparkling color slides illustrate it with a beauty that tugs at your heart and sets your heels to itching just a little. You owe yourself the pleasure of this book."

—*Biloxi (Mississippi) Sun Herald*

"It is soul reading—the simplicity of a man's inner feelings stated in terms which leave no misunderstandings.... A classic of its kind."

—*Lansing (Michigan) State Journal*

"A simply written book.... I finished it in just a few nights, and was sorry when I did."

—*Gary (Indiana) Post-Tribune*

"Many of us will never realize the dream of such an escape from our hectic, complex life to that of the solitude of the wilderness. But in the pages of this book we can share with a man who lived his dream. The book is certain to bring much pleasure to anyone who loves the outdoors."

—*Portsmouth (Ohio) Times*

"This is the record of a man in our own time who went into the bush. It is the story of a dream shared by many, fulfilled by few, brought into sharp focus by the beautiful color photographs and the simple account of Proenneke's life."

—*Burlington (Vermont) Free Press*

"A gorgeous picture story of one man's adventure in the remote Twin Lakes area, where he built a cabin and overcame nature's challenges."

—*Cleveland (Ohio) Plain Dealer*

One Man's Wilderness

One Man's Wilderness

◆

AN ALASKAN ODYSSEY

By Sam Keith from the Journals
and Photographs of Richard Proenneke

ALASKA NORTHWEST BOOKS®

ANCHORAGE ▪ PORTLAND

Text © by Sam Keith and Richard Proenneke
Photographs © by Richard Proenneke
Book compilation © 1999 by Alaska Northwest Books®
An Imprint of Graphic Arts Center Publishing Company
P.O. Box 10306, Portland, Oregon 97296-0306, 503-226-2402

Eighth Alaska Northwest Books® printing 2004

Library of Congress Cataloging-in-Publication Data

Proenneke, Richard
    One man's wilderness : an Alaskan odyssey / by Sam Keith ; from the journals and
    photograph collection of Richard Proenneke. - 26th anniversary ed.
         p.   cm.
    Originally published: Anchorage : Alaska Northwest Pub. Co. [1973]
    ISBN 0-88240-513-6
    1. Proenneke, Richard—Diaries. 2. Pioneers—Alaska—Twin Lakes Region (north of Lake
Clark)—Diaries. 3. Twin Lakes Region (Alaska)—Description and travel. 4. Twin Lakes
Region (Alaska)—Pictorial works. 5. Frontier and pioneer life—Alaska—Twin Lakes Region
6. Wilderness survival—Alaska—Twin Lakes Region I. Keith, Sam. II. Title.
F912.T85P76   1999
917.98'4-dc21   98-27704
                                                                                      CIP

President/Publisher: Charles M. Hopkins
Editorial Staff: Douglas A. Pfeiffer, Ellen Harkins Wheat, Timothy W. Frew, Diana S. Eilers,
    Jean Andrews, Alicia I. Paulson, Deborah J. Loop, Joanna M. Goebel
Production Staff: Richard L. Owsiany, Susan Dupere
Designer: Elizabeth Watson
Map: Gray Mouse Graphics
Illustrator: Roz Pape
Photographer: Richard Proenneke
Cover Photos: Richard Proenneke
Printed in the United States of America

– Preface –

Although Dick Proenneke came originally from Primrose, Iowa, he will always be to me as truly Alaskan as willow brush and pointed spruce and jagged peaks against the sky. He embodies the spirit of the "Great Land."

I met Dick in 1952 when I worked as a civilian on the Kodiak Naval Base. Together we explored the many wild bays of Kodiak and Afognak Islands where the giant brown bear left his tracks in the black sand, climbed mountains to the clear lakes hidden beyond their green shoulders, gorged ourselves on fat butter clams steamed over campfires that flickered before shelters of driftwood and saplings of spruce.

It was during these times that I observed and admired his wonderful gift of patience, his exceptional ability to improvise, his unbelievable stamina, and his consuming curiosity of all that was around him. Here was a remarkable blending of mechanical aptitude and genuine love of the natural scene, and even though I often saw him crawling over the complex machinery of the twentieth century, his coveralls smeared with grease, I always envisioned him in buckskins striding through the high mountain passes in the days of Lewis and Clark.

If a tough job had to be done, Dick was the man to do it. A tireless worker, his talents as a diesel mechanic were not only in demand on the base but eagerly sought by the contractors in town. His knowledge, his imagination, and his tenacity were more than stubborn machinery could resist.

His quiet efficiency fascinated me. I wondered about the days before he came to Alaska.

While performing his duties as a carpenter in the U.S. Navy during World War II, he was stricken with rheumatic fever. For six months he was bedridden. It kept him from shipping out into the fierce action that awaited in the Pacific, but more than anything else, it made him despise this weakness of his body that had temporarily disabled him. Once recovered, he set about proving to himself again and again that this repaired machine was going to outperform all others. He drove himself beyond common endurance. This former failing of his body became an obsession, and he mercilessly put it to the test at every opportunity.

After the war he went to diesel school. He could have remained there as an instructor, but yearnings from the other side of his nature had to be answered. He worked on a ranch as a sheep camp tender in the high lonesome places of Oregon. As the result of a friend's urging and the prospect of starting a cattle ranch on Shuyak Island, he came to Alaska in 1950.

This dream soon vanished when the island proved unsuitable for the venture. A visit to a cattle spread on Kodiak further convinced the would-be partners that, for the time being at least, the Alaska ranch idea was out. They decided to go their separate ways.

For several years Dick worked as a heavy equipment operator and repairman on the naval base at Kodiak. He worked long, hard hours in all kinds of weather for construction contractors. He fished commercially for salmon. He worked for the Fish and Wildlife Service at King Salmon on the Alaska Peninsula. And though his living for the most part came from twisting bolts and welding steel, his heart was always in those faraway peaks that lost themselves in the clouds.

A turning point in Dick's life came when a retired Navy captain who had a cabin in a remote wilderness area invited Dick to spend a few weeks with him and his wife. They had to fly in over the Alaska Range. This was Dick's introduction to the Twin Lakes country, and he knew the day he left it that one day he would return.

The return came sooner than he expected. He was working for a contractor who was being pressured by union officials to hire only union men. Dick always felt he was his own man. His philosophy was simple: Do the job you must do and don't worry about the hours or the conditions.

Here was the excuse Dick needed. He was fifty years old. Why not retire? He could afford the move.

"Get yourself off the hook," he told the contractor. "That brush beyond the big hump has been calling for a long time and maybe I better answer while I'm able."

That was in the spring of 1967.

He spent the following summer and fall in the Navy captain's cabin at Twin Lakes. Scouting the area thoroughly, he finally selected his site and planned in detail the building of his cabin. In late July he cut his logs from a stand of white spruce, hauled them out of the timber, peeled them, piled them, and left them to weather through the harsh winter. Babe Alsworth, the bush pilot, flew him out just before freeze-up.

Dick returned to Iowa to see his folks and do his customary good deeds around the small town. There in the "flatlander" country he awaited the rush of spring. He had cabin logs on his mind. His ears were tuned for the clamoring of the geese that would send him north again.

Here is the account of a man living in an area as yet unspoiled by man's advance, a land with all the purity that the land around us once held. Here is the account of a man living in a place where no roads lead in or out, where the nearest settlement is forty air miles over a rugged land spined with mountains, mattressed with muskeg, and gashed with river torrents.

Using Dick Proenneke's rough journals as a guide, and knowing him as well as I did, I have tried to get into his mind and reveal the "flavor" of the man. This is my tribute to him, a celebration of his being in tune with his surroundings and what he did alone with simple tools and ingenuity in carving his masterpiece out of the beyond.

Sam Keith
Duxbury, Massachusetts (1973)

~ Contents ~

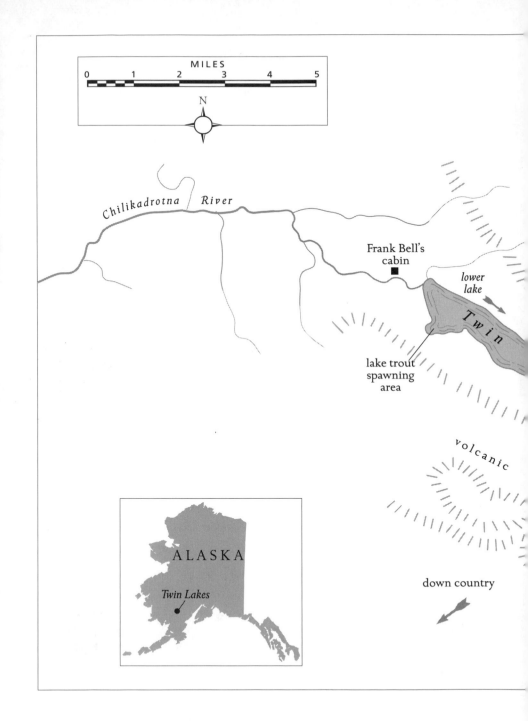

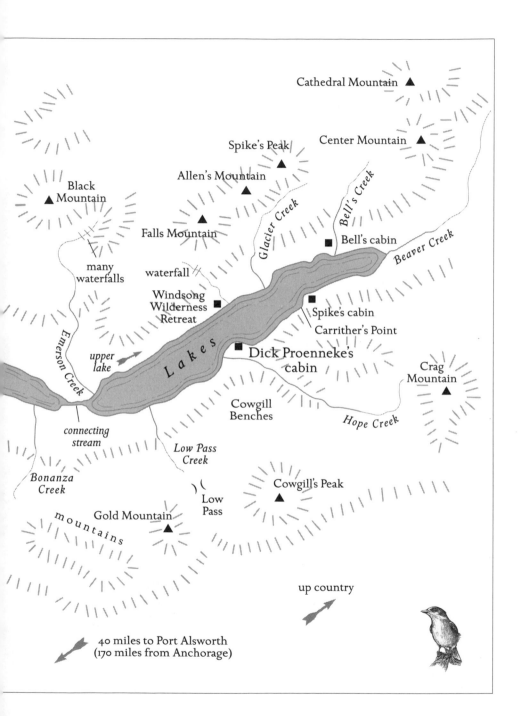

Cathedral Mountain ▲

Center Mountain ▲

Spike's Peak
▲

Allen's Mountain
▲

Bell's cabin ■

Black
▲ Mountain

Falls Mountain
▲

Glacier Creek

Bell's Creek

Beaver Creek

many
waterfalls

waterfall

Windsong
Wilderness
Retreat ■

Spike's cabin ■

Carrither's Point

Lakes

■ Dick Proenneke's
cabin

Crag
Mountain ▲

Emerson Creek

upper
lake

Cowgill
Benches

Hope Creek

connecting
stream

*Low Pass
Creek*

*Bonanza
Creek*

Cowgill's Peak
▲

m o u n t a i n s

Gold Mountain
▲

Low
Pass

up country

40 miles to Port Alsworth
(170 miles from Anchorage)

I'm Scared of It All

I'm scared of it all, God's truth! so I am
It's too big and brutal for me.
My nerve's on the raw and I don't give a damn
For all the "hoorah" that I see.
I'm pinned between subway and overhead train,
Where automobillies sweep down:
Oh, I want to go back to the timber again . . .
I'm scared of the terrible town.

I want to go back to my lean, ashen plains;
My rivers that flash into foam;
My ultimate valleys where solitude reigns;
My trail from Fort Churchill to Nome.
My forests packed full of mysterious gloom,
My ice fields agrind and aglare:
The city is deadfalled with danger and doom . . .
I know that I'm safer up there.

I watch the wan faces that flash in the street;
All kinds and all classes I see.
Yet never a one in the million I meet,
Has the smile of a comrade to me.
Just jaded and panting like dogs in a pack;
Just tensed and intent on the goal:
O God! but I'm lonesome . . . I wish I was back,
Up there in the land of the Pole.

I feel it's all wrong, but I can't tell you why ...
The palace, the hovel next door;
The insolent towers that sprawl to the sky,
The crush and the rush and the roar.
I'm trapped like a fox and I fear for my pelt;
I cower in the crash and the glare;
Oh, I want to be back in the avalanche belt,
For I know that it's safer up there!

I'm scared of it all: Oh, afar I can hear
The voice of the solitudes call!
We're nothing but brute with a little veneer,
And nature is best after all.
There's tumult and terror abroad in the street;
There's menace and doom in the air;
I've got to get back to my thousand mile beat;
The trail where the cougar and silvertip meet;
The snows and the campfire, with wolves at my feet ...
    Goodbye, for it's safer up there.

From "Rhymes of a Rolling Stone," by Robert W. Service.
Reprinted by permission of Dodd Mead and Company,
from the collected poems of Robert Service.

– Going In –

I recognized the scrawl. I eased the point of a knife blade into the flap and slit open the envelope. It was the letter at last from Babe Alsworth, the bush pilot. "Come anytime. If we can't land on the ice with wheels, we can find some open water for floats." Typical Babe. Not a man to waste his words.

This meant the end of my stay with Spike and Hope Carrithers at Sawmill Lake on Kodiak. I had driven my camper north and was doing odd jobs for them while waiting to hear from Babe. Their cabin in the Twin Lakes region had fired me up for the wilderness adventure I was about to go on. They seemed to sense my excitement and restlessness. I could use their cabin until I built one of my own. I could use their tools and was taking in more of my own. I also had the use of their Grumman canoe to travel up and down twelve miles of water as clear as a dewdrop.

I left my camper in their care. I waved to them as I heard the engines begin to roar, and then the land moved faster and faster as I hurtled down the Kodiak strip on the flight to Anchorage. Babe would meet me there.

■ *May 17, 1968.* At Merrill Field, while waiting for Babe to drop out of the sky in his 180 Cessna, I squinted at the Chugach Range, white and glistening in the sun, and I thought about the trip back north in the camper. It was always a good feeling to be heading north. In a Nebraska town I had bought a felt-tipped

marker and on the back of my camper I printed in big letters, DESTINATION—
BACK AND BEYOND. It was really surprising how many cars pulled up behind and
stayed close for a minute or two even though the way was clear for passing.
Then as they passed, a smile, a wave, or a wistful look that said more than words
could. Westward to the Oregon ranch country and those high green places
where I had worked in the 1940s. On to Seattle where a modern freeway led me
through the city without a stop, and I thought of the grizzled old lumberjack
who bragged that he had cut timber on First and Pike. Hard to imagine those
tall virgin stands of Douglas fir and cedar and hemlock in place of cement,
steel, and asphalt. Then the Cariboo Highway and beautiful British Columbia.
Smack into a blizzard as I crossed Pine Pass on the John Hart Highway to
Dawson Creek. And all those other places with their wonderful names: Muncho
Lake and Teslin and Whitehorse, Kluane and Tok Junction, Matanuska and the
Kenai. The ferry ride across the wild Gulf of Alaska and a red sun sinking into
the rich blue of it. Sawmill Lake, and now Anchorage.

The weather stayed clear, and Babe was on time. Same old Babe. Short in
body and tall on experience. Wiry as a weasel. Sharp featured. Blue eyes that
glinted from beneath eyebrows that tufted like feathers. A gray stubble of a
moustache. That stocking cap perched atop his head. A real veteran of the bush.
"Watches the weather," his son-in-law once told me. "He knows the signs. If
they're not to his liking he'll just sit by the fire and wait on better ones. That's
why he's been around so long."

"Smooth through the pass," Babe said. "A few things to pick up in town and
we're on our way."

We did the errands and returned to load our cargo aboard the 180. Babe
got his clearance and off we went, Babe seeming to look over a hood that was
too high for him. A banking turn over the outskirts of Anchorage, then we
were droning over the mud flats of Cook Inlet on the 170 air-mile trip to Port
Alsworth on Lake Clark. I looked down on the muskeg meadows pockmarked
with puddles and invaded by stringy ranks of spruce. Now and then I glanced at
Babe, whose eyes seemed transfixed on the entrance to Lake Clark Pass, his

chin resting in one cupped hand. Meditating as usual. I searched the ground below for a moose, but we were too high to see enough detail.

Suddenly the mountains hemmed us in on either side—steep wooded shoulders and ribs of rock falling away to the river that flowed to the south below, here and there a thin waterfall that appeared and disappeared in streamers of mist. We tossed in the air currents. Then we were above the big glacier, dirty with earth and boulders yet glinting blue from its shadowed crevices. It looked as though we were passing over the blades of huge, upturned axes, and then the land began to drop dizzily away beneath us and we were over the summit. The glacial river below was now flowing in a northerly direction through a dense forest of spruce, dividing now and then past slender islands of silt, and merging again in its rush to Lake Clark.

There it was, a great silvery area in the darkness of the spruce—Lake Clark. We came in low over the water, heading for Tanalian Point and Babe's place at Port Alsworth. Years ago he had decided to settle here because it was a natural layover for bush pilots flying from Kachemak Bay and Cook Inlet through Lake Clark Pass to Bristol Bay. It had been a good move and a good living.

I spotted the wind sock on the mast above the greenhouse and glanced at my watch. The trip had taken an hour and a half. Down we slanted to touch down on the stony strip. On the taxi in we hit a soft place, and we wound up hauling our cargo of baby chicks, groceries, and gear in a wheelbarrow over the mud to the big house.

I helped Babe the next few days. We patched the roof of his house. We put a new nose cowl on the Taylorcraft, attached the floats, and there she was, all poised to take me over the mountains on a thirty-minute flight to journey's end.

■ *May 21st.* Mares' tails in the sky. A chance of a change in the fine weather and probably wind that could hold me at Port Alsworth until the storm passed over. I had been delayed long enough. Even Mary Alsworth's cooking could hold me no longer. Babe sensed my itchiness. He squinted at the mountains and gave his silent approval.

We loaded my gear into the T-craft. Not too many groceries this trip; Babe would come again soon. Seemed like a heavy load to me, and jammed in as we were, I found myself wondering whether the old bird could get off the water. We taxied out, rippling the reflections of the sky and the mountains. The motor shuddered and roared, and I watched the spray plume away from the floats. We lifted easily toward the peaks and home.

Below us a wild land heaved with mountains and was gashed deep with valleys. I could see game trails in the snow. Most of the high lakes were frozen over. I was counting on open water where the upper lake dumped into the lower, but the Twins were 2,200 feet higher above sea level than Lake Clark and could still be sealed up tight.

We broke out over the lower lake to find most of it white with ice. There was open water where the connecting stream spilled in, enough to land in. The upper lake had a greenish cast but only traces of open water along the edges. We circled Spike's cabin. Everything looked to be in good shape, so we returned to the open spot of water on the lower lake. I would have to pack my gear the three and a half miles along the shore to the cabin. As we sloped in for a landing, a dozen or more diving ducks flurried trails over the water and labored their plump bodies into the air.

After unloading, Babe and I sat on the beach.

"This is truly God's country," I said, my eyes roving above the spruce tips to the high peaks.

Babe said nothing for a few minutes. He was lost in thought. "Compared to heaven," he said finally, "this is a dung hill." He rubbed a forefinger against the stubble of his moustache and pushed the watch cap farther back on his head. "Nothing but a dung hill."

I looked at the water, at the stones on the bottom as sharply etched as if seen through a fine camera lens. "This is as close as I hope to get to heaven," I said. "This is here and now. Something I'm sure of. How can heaven be any better than this?"

Babe's eyebrows seemed to lift like crests. "Man!" he spluttered. "Man, you don't know what you're talking about! Your philosophy worries me. Why, it says plain in the Bible...."

I knew he would get me around to his favorite subject sooner or later. "One life at a time," I said. "If there's another one—well, that's a bonus. And I'm not so sure of that next one."

Babe shook his head sorrowfully. "You better think on it," he muttered, rising to his feet. "You'll have a lot of time to do just that." He waded out, stepped up on a float, and squinted at me over his shoulder. "Man, your philosophy...."

I pushed the plane toward deeper water. The T-craft coughed and stuttered into a smooth idling. Babe craned out the side hatch. He wondered, would the lake be open in a week? Ten days? He would be back inside of two weeks.

I watched him take off like a giant loon. He was really banking a lot on heaven. He said he was ready for the Lord to take him anytime. He was even looking forward to it. I just hoped that when the time came he wouldn't be disappointed. I watched him until the speck went out of sight over the volcanic mountains.

It was good to be back in the wilderness again where everything seems at peace. I was alone. It was a great feeling—a stirring feeling. Free once more to plan and do as I pleased. Beyond was all around me. The dream was a dream no longer.

I suppose I was here because this was something I had to do. Not just dream about it but do it. I suppose, too, I was here to test myself, not that I had never done it before, but this time it was to be a more thorough and lasting examination.

What was I capable of that I didn't know yet? What about my limits? Could I truly enjoy my own company for an entire year? Was I equal to everything this wild land could throw at me? I had seen its moods in late spring, summer, and early fall, but what about winter? Would I love the isolation then, with its bone-stabbing cold, its brooding ghostly silence, its forced confinement? At age fifty-one I intended to find out.

My mind was swarming with the how and when of projects. Could I really build the cabin with just hand tools to the standards I had set in my mind? The furniture, the doors, the windows—what was the best way to produce the needed boards? Would the tin gas cans serve as I hoped they would? Was the fireplace too ambitious a project? The cabin had to be ready before summer's end, but the cache up on its poles? Surely that must wait until next spring. There were priorities to establish and deadlines to meet. I would need the extra daylight the summer would bring.

The most exciting part of the whole adventure was putting self-reliance on trial. I did not intend to break any laws. No meat would be harvested until hunting season. Until then fish would be a mainstay of my diet, along with berries and wild greens. I would plant a small garden more out of curiosity than actual need. Babe would supply those extras that provide a little luxury to daily fare. He would be my one contact with that other world beyond the range.

I looked around at the wind-blasted peaks and the swirls of mist moving past them. It was hard to take my eyes away. I had been up on some of them, and I would be up there again. There was something different to see each time, and something different from each one. All those streamlets to explore and all those tracks to follow through the glare of the high basins and over the saddles. Where did they lead? What was beyond? What stories were written in the snow?

I watched an eagle turn slowly and fall away, quick-sliding across the dark stands of spruce that marched in uneven ranks up the slopes. His piercing cry came back on the wind. I thought of the man at his desk staring down from a city window at the ant colony streets below, the man toiling beside the thudding and rumbling of machinery, the man commuting to his job the same way at the same time each morning, staring at but not seeing the poles and the wires and the dirty buildings flashing past. Perhaps each man had his moment during the day when his vision came, a vision not unlike the one before me.

A strange possessiveness seemed to surge through me. I had no right to call this big country mine, yet I felt it was.

I examined my heap of gear on the gravel. There were 150 pounds to be backpacked along the connecting stream and the upper shoreline to Spike's cabin. Many times I had gone over in my mind what to take. I knew what was available in the cabin but didn't want to use any more of Spike's gear or supplies than I had to. Things were valuable out here and hard to replace. Spread before me were the essentials. I organized the array into three loads.

I was sure I could pack two loads today, but just in case it was only one, I included in the first trip a .30-06 converted Army Springfield, a box of cartridges, a .357 magnum pistol with cartridge belt and holster, the packboard, the camera gear (8mm movie and 35mm reflex), cartons of film, the foodstuffs (oatmeal, powdered milk, flour, salt, pepper, sugar, honey, rice, onions, baking soda, dehydrated potatoes, dried fruit, a few tins of butter, half a slab of bacon), and a jar of Mary Alsworth's ageless sourdough starter.

The second pile consisted of binoculars, spotting scope, tripod, a double-bitted axe, fishing gear, a sleeping bag, packages of seeds, *A Field Guide to Western Birds*, my ten-inch pack, and the clothing. More bulk than weight.

The third pile held the hand tools such as wood augers, files, chisels, drawknife, saws, saw set, honing stone, vise grips, screwdrivers, adze, plumb bob and line, string level, square, chalk, chalk line, and carpenter pencils; a galvanized pail containing such things as masking tape, nails, sheet metal screws, haywire, clothesline, needles and thread, wooden matches, a magnifying glass, and various repair items; a bag of plaster of Paris; and some oakum.

Over the last two piles I spread the tarp and weighted its edges with boulders. Then I shouldered the first load, buckled on the .357, slung up the rifle and went off, swishing through the buckbrush with the enthusiasm of a Boy Scout setting out on his first hike.

The stream tinkled as it moved past its ice chimes. I saw an arctic tern dipping its way along the open place where the stream poured from beneath the ice. A wren-type bird kept flushing and flitting daintily ahead of me. His tiny body had a yellowish green cast to it, but he wouldn't sit still long enough for me to catch a good field mark.

A thin film of ice covered yesterday's open water between the edge of the lake ice and the shore. There had been a dip in the temperature last night. It was tricky going as I picked my way with quick steps over the patches of snow and ice and through stretches of great boulders and loose gravel. The pull of the packboard straps felt comfortable against my woolen shirt, and I could feel the warmth of the spring sun on my face. I wondered if at that moment there was anyone in the world as free and happy.

I crossed the single-log bridge over Hope Creek. Another hundred yards and I broke out of the brush to my pile of cabin logs. At first glance, disappointment. They seemed badly checked, but they were going to have to do. I leaned against them, resting the packboard, and took a little parcel wrapped in wax paper from a pocket. It was a piece of smoked sockeye salmon, a sample from some Babe had in the T-craft. Squaw candy, the Natives called it. I bit off a chunk. It was rich with flavor, and while I chewed, my eyes wandered over the peeled logs.

That had been a big job last July, hard work but I enjoyed it. It was cool in the timber, and there were mornings I could see my breath. I had harvested the logs from a stand of spruce less than 300 yards from where they were now piled. The trees could have been dropped with a saw but I chose to use a double-bitted axe. Pulling a canoe paddle through miles of lakes had put me in shape for the work.

Learn to use an axe and respect it and you can't help but love it. Abuse one and it will wear your hands raw and open your foot like an overcooked sausage. Each blade was nursed to a perfect edge, and the keenness of its bright arc made my strokes more accurate and more deliberate. No sloppy moves with that deadly beauty! Before I started on a tree I carefully cleared obstructions that might tangle in the backswing. It was fun planning where each should fall, and notching it for direction. *Snuck! Snuck!* The ax made a solid sound as it bit deeply into the white wood.

There is a pride in blending each stroke into the slash. A deft twist now and then to pop a heavy piece from the cut. Downward swipes followed by one from a flatter angle, the white gash growing larger as chips leap out and fall on the moss of the forest floor. Then the attack on the other side, the tree tipping slowly toward the aisle selected, gaining momentum, hitting with a crash. Moving along its fallen length, slicing off the limbs close to the trunk.

Then the peeling. Easier than expected. A spruce pole tapered into a wedge-like blade was worked under the bark until the layer gave way to expose the wet naked wood. Then the hauling. Green, peeled trunks, some of them twenty-footers, had to be moved to the site. I fashioned a log dragger. It was nothing more than a pole like a wagon tongue, a gas-can tin shoe on the end fastened to the log butt with a spike, a crossbar on the other. Back up to the rig like a horse, grab the crossbar in both fists, and take off with legs driving. The log, all slippery with sap, skidded over the moss, and with bent back I kept it going until I reached the piling place.

The sharp smell of spruce in the air, the rushing, powerful noises of the creek, the fit feeling of blood surging through the muscles. That was the way it was with all fifty of them. About a week's work—real bull work but I never felt any better. Folks say that axemanship is a lost art, but I like to think I found it again in those cool spruce woods.

The logs were a great deal lighter now than they were then and could be handled easily enough. I wrapped the smoked salmon in the wax paper and put it back in a pocket. It was time to be moving on. I was anxious to get to Spike's cabin to see if it was the way I had left it last September. About 500 yards more through the spruce and the willow brush and there it was, its weather-grayed moose antlers spreading just below the peak of the roof, a tin can cover on its stovepipe, and its windows boarded up. It had a lonesome, forlorn look. It needed someone to live in it.

I lifted the bar of the cabin door and pushed inside. Close quarters with the canoe in there. Spike's note was still a prominent part of the entrance. It read, "Use things as you need them. Leave things as you found them." From the looks of the place no one had been inside. If anyone had, he had been very neat about it.

The cabin had everything needed to set up housekeeping until my own place was completed. A good stove, two bunks, a roof that didn't leak, a table, and a small supply of cooking staples and the necessary tools to go with them. A small stack of dry wood inside, in addition to the supply outside that I had cut last fall. When my cabin was ready and moving day was at hand, I would leave behind a little more than I had found.

Including the brief stop at the log pile, the trip had taken an hour and three quarters. Not bad time with a load. I unslung the ought-six and set down the packboard. My shoulders felt as though they wanted to float to the rafters.

First thing was to move the Grumman canoe outside and make some room. Next I uncovered the windows to get rid of the gloom and climbed a ladder to take the tin can off the top of the stovepipe. When I got back with the second load, I would make a fire.

If I could travel the lake ice, I would use the canoe like a sled. I shoved the canoe onto the ice and found it was too rotten and thin. A strong wind would break it up. It was back along the beach the way I had come.

My second load was about sixty pounds. I huddled together what was left and spread the tarp over it, again weighting the edges with boulders. If the weather changed, the gear would be well protected. This time with the binoculars along, I would have an excuse to stop now and then and glass the slopes for game. With the naked eye you don't often see the big animals unless they are fairly close, and might think there are none in the country. Through the lenses, with the high slopes drawn into sharp definition, you can spot movement or something that changes shade.

On Black Mountain I saw six Dall sheep. Farther on against the skyline of Falls Mountain, there was a big band with lambs among them. Just before crossing the log bridge on Hope Creek I spotted a lone caribou feeding along the Cowgill Benches. I could make out the stubs of new antlers. As I plodded along I knew many eyes were watching me. Was the word being passed that I was back?

At the cabin, once more unloaded, I opened a jar of blueberries I had picked and put up in September. The winter had been hard on them. Juice was two-thirds the way up the jar with the shriveled berries on top. They had a strong aroma and a sharp taste.

I decided to save the last load for morning. I distributed what I had brought so far into readily available places. I placed the ought-six on wall pegs. I didn't figure on getting the barrel dirty for a long time.

With the fire going, the cabin took on a cheery atmosphere. A few fat flies awakened and buzzed about sluggishly. When I went outside to get an armload of wood, I stopped to look at the thin blue smoke pluming against the green darkness of the spruce. It began to look and feel like home.

Supper was caribou sandwiches Mary Alsworth had packed, washed down with a cup of hot beef bouillon. Then I got ready for morning. I uncovered the jar of sourdough starter, dumped two-thirds of it into a bowl, put three heaping teaspoons of flour back into the starter jar, added some lukewarm water, stirred and capped it. If I did this every time, the starter would go on forever.

To the starter in the bowl I added five tablespoons of flour, three table-spoons of sugar, and a half cup of dry milk, mixing it all together with a wooden spoon. I dribbled in lukewarm water until the batter was thin. Then I covered the bowl with a pan. The mixture would work itself into a hotcake batter by morning.

Babe did me a real favor flying me in today. I hope he's a better businessman with others. He's never yet charged me the going rate of $30 for his mail and grocery runs from Port Alsworth to Twin Lakes. He makes me feel like it would be an insult to question him about the price. "We are not piling up treasures on this earth," he says. I hope I can make up the difference in other ways.

My first evening was clear and calm. I wish some of those folks who passed me in my camper and waved could see this place. Mosquitoes are out and working on the sunburn I acquired while packing this afternoon. Listen to them singing a tune. Brings to mind a comment Babe made one time. "Can't be very good country," he said, "when even a mosquito wouldn't live there." By the sound I allow this is prime country. I wonder if there are any mosquitoes in heaven.

– *The Birth of a Cabin* –

■ *May 22nd.* Up with the sun at four to watch the sunrise and the sight of the awakening land. It seems a shame for eyes to be shut when such things are going on, especially in this big country. I don't want to miss anything. A heavy white frost twinkled almost as if many of its crystals were suspended in the air. New ice, like a thin pane of glass, sealed the previously open water along the edge of the lake. The peaks, awash in the warm yellow light, contrasted sharply with their slopes still in shadow.

Soon I had a fire snapping in the stove, and shortly afterward could no longer see my breath inside the cabin. A pan of water was heating alongside the kettle. That business of breaking a hole in the ice and washing up out there sounds better than it feels. I prefer warm water and soap. Does a better job, too.

Thick bacon sliced from the slab sizzled in the black skillet. I poured off some of the fat and put it aside to cool. Time now to put the finishing touches to the sourdough batter. As I uncovered it I could smell the fermentation. I gave it a good stirring, then sprinkled half a teaspoonful of baking soda on top, scattered a pinch of salt, and dripped in a tablespoon of bacon fat. When these additions were gently folded into the batter, it seemed to come alive. I let it stand for a few minutes while bacon strips were laid on a piece of paper towel and excess fat was drained from the pan. Then I dropped one wooden spoonful of batter, hissing onto the skillet. When bubbles appear all over, it's time to flip.

Brown, thin, and light—nothing quite like a stack of sourdough hotcakes cooked over a wood fire in the early morning. I smeared each layer with butter and honey and topped the heap with lean bacon slices. While I ate I peered out the window at a good-looking caribou bedded down on the upper benches. Now that's a breakfast with atmosphere!

Before doing the dishes, I readied the makings of the sourdough biscuits. These would be a must for each day's supper. The recipe is much the same as for hotcakes, but thicker, a dough that is baked.

It was a good morning to pack in the rest of the gear. I put some red beans in a pot to soak and took off. Last night's freeze had crusted the snow, and it made the traveling easier. About a mile down the lakeshore a cock ptarmigan clattered out of the willow brush, his neck and head shining a copper color in the sun, his white wings vibrating, then curving into a set as he sailed. His summer plumage was beginning to erase the white of winter. *Crrr . . . uck . . . a . . . ruck . . . urrrrrrrrr.* His ratcheting call must have brought everything on the mountain slopes to attention.

The last load was the heaviest. It was almost noon before I got back to the cabin, and none too soon because rain clouds were gathering over the mountains to the south.

The rain came slanting down, hard-driven by the wind. I busied myself getting gear and groceries organized. Anyone living alone has to get things down to a system—know where things are and what the next move is going to be. Chores are easier if forethought is given to them and they are looked upon as little pleasures to perform instead of inconveniences that steal time and try the patience.

When the rain stopped its heavy pelting, I went prospecting for a garden site. A small clearing on the south side of the cabin and away from the big trees was the best place I could find. Here it would get as much sun as possible.

Frost was only inches down, so there would be no planting until June. Spike's grub hoe could scuff off the ground cover later on and stir up the top soil as deep as the frost would permit. I had no fertilizer. I suppose I might experiment with the manure of moose and caribou, but it would be interesting to see what progress foreign seeds would make in soil that had nourished only native plants.

By suppertime the biscuits were nicely puffed and ready to bake. There was no oven in the stove, but with tinsnips I cut down a coffee can so it stood about two inches high, and placed it bottomside up atop the stove. On this platform I set the pan of three swollen biscuits and covered it with a gas can tin about six inches deep.

In about fifteen minutes the smell of the biscuits drifted out to the woodpile. I parked the axe in the chopping block. Inside, I dampened a towel and spread it over the biscuits for about two minutes to tenderize the crust. The last biscuit mopped up what was left of the onion gravy. _Mmmm._

When will I ever tire of just looking? I set up the spotting scope on the tripod. Three different eyepieces fit into it: a 25-power, a 40-power, and a 60-power. That last one hauls distant objects right up to you, but it takes a while to get the knack of using it because the magnification field covers a relatively small area.

This evening's main attraction was a big lynx moving across a snow patch. I had seen a sudden flurrying of ptarmigan just moments before, and when I trained the scope on the action, there was the cat taking his time, stopping now and then as if watching for a movement in the timber just ahead of him.

I switched to a more powerful eyepiece and there he was again, bigger and better, strolling along, his hips seeming to be higher than his shoulders, his body the color of dark gray smoke, his eyes like yellow lanterns beneath his tufted ears. Even from the distance I could sense his big-footed silence.

I went to sleep wondering if the lynx had ptarmigan for supper.

■ _May 23rd._ Dense fog this morning. A ghostly scene. Strange how much bigger things appear in the fog. A pair of goldeneye ducks whistled past low and looked as big as honkers to me.

After breakfast I inspected the red beans for stones, dumped them into a fresh pot of water from the lake, and let them bubble for a spell on the stove. I sliced some onions. What in the world would I do without onions? I read one time that they prevent blood clots. Can't afford a blood clot out here. I threw the slices into the beans by the handful, showered in some chili powder and salt, and stirred in a thick stream of honey. I left the pot to simmer over a slow fire. Come suppertime they should be full of flavor.

I took a tour back through the spruce timber. It didn't take much detective work to see how hard the wind had blown during the winter, both up and down the lake. Trees were down in both directions. That was something else to think about. Did the wind blow that much harder in the winter?

Hope Creek has cut a big opening into the lake ice. That could be where the ducks were headed this morning. Was it too early to catch a fish? I took the casting rod along to find out. The creek mouth looked promising enough with its ruffled water swirling into eddies that spun beneath the ice barrier. I worked a metal spoon deep in the current, jerked it toward me and let it drift back. Not a strike after several casts. If the fish were out there, they were not interested. No sign of the ducks either.

When the fog finally cleared the face of the mountain across the ice, I sighted a bunch of eleven Dall ewes and lambs. Five lambs in all, a good sign. A mountain has got to be lonely without sheep on it.

The rest of the day I devoted to my tools. I carved a mallet head out of a spruce chunk, augered a hole in it, and fitted a handle to it. This would be a useful pounding tool, and I hadn't had to pack it in either. The same with the handles I made for the wood augers, the wide-bladed chisel, and the files— much easier to pack without the handles already fitted to them.

I sharpened the axe, adze, saws, chisels, wood augers, drawknife, pocket knife, and bacon slicer. The whispering an oil stone makes against steel is a satisfying sound. You can almost tell when the blade is ready by the crispness of the sound. A keen edge not only does a better job, it teaches a man to have respect for the tool. There is no leeway for a "small" slip.

While I pampered my assault kit for the building of the cabin, the sky turned loose a heavy shower and thundered Midwestern style. The echoes rumbled and tumbled down the slopes and faded away into mutterings. The shrill cries of the terns proclaimed their confusion.

The ice attempted to move today. Fog and thunder have taken their toll. I can see the rough slab edges pushed atop each other along the cracks. The winter freight will be moving down the lake soon, through the connecting stream and down the lower lake to the funnel of the Chilikadrotna River.

After supper I made log-notch markers out of my spruce stock. They are nothing more than a pair of dividers with a pencil on one leg, but with them I can make logs fit snugly. This is not going to be a butchering job. I can afford the time for pride to stay in charge.

I sampled the red beans again before turning in for the night. The longer they stay in the pot the more flavor they have.

The woodpile needs attention. I must drop a few spruce snags and buck them up into sections. Dry standing timber makes the best firewood.

Ho, hum. I'm anxious to get started on that cabin, but first things first. Tomorrow will have to be a woodcutting day.

• _May 25th._ The mountains are wearing new hats this morning. The rain during the night was snow at the higher levels.

I built up the wood supply yesterday and this morning. There is a rhythm to the saw as its teeth eat back and forth in the deepening cut, but I must admit I enjoy the splitting more. To hit the chunk exactly where you want to and cleave it apart cleanly—there's a good sound to it and satisfaction in an efficient motion. Another reward comes from seeing those triangular stove lengths pile up. Then the grand finale! Drive the ax into the block, look around, and contemplate the measure of what you have done.

Breakup was not the spectacular sight it was last year. A big wind would have cleared the thin ice out yesterday. As I loaded tools on the packboard this afternoon, the rotted ice began to flow past in quiet exit.

At the construction site several hundred yards down the lakeshore, I found my logs were not as badly checked as I had first thought. The checking was only evident on the weathered sides. The logs were well seasoned and light in weight for their length.

When you have miles and miles of lakefront and picture views to consider, it is difficult to select a building site. The more a man looks, the fussier he gets. I had given much thought to mine. It sat atop a knoll about seventy-five feet back from a bight in the shoreline. There was a good beach for landing a canoe, and a floatplane also could be brought in there easily.

The wind generally blew up or down the lake. From either direction the cabin would be screened by spruce trees and willow brush. The knoll was elevated well above any visible high-water marks. Just over 100 yards away was Hope Creek, and even though the water from the lake was sweet and pure, Hope Creek carried the best ever from the high places. At its mouth could usually be found fish, too.

There were two things that bothered me just a little, and I gave them serious consideration before making the final decision. It was possible that after a continuous heavy rain and the resulting runoff from the mountains, Hope Creek could overflow and come churning through the timber behind me. If that happened, I felt I was still high enough to handle the situation. Perhaps some engineering would be necessary to divert the flow until the creek tamed down and returned to its channel.

It was also a possibility, though quite remote, that a slide or a quake might choke the Chilikadrotna River, which was the drainpipe of the Twins. Anytime the volume of water coming into the country was greater than what was going out, the lake level was going to rise. If the Chilikadrotna were to plug seriously, the country would fill up like a giant bathtub. I didn't like to think about that. Finally I decided such a catastrophe would rule out any site, and if a man had to consider all of nature's knockout punches, he would hesitate to build anywhere.

So I had taken the plunge and cleared the brush. I had grubbed out a shallow foundation, had hauled up beach gravel and had spread it to a depth of several inches over an area roughly twenty feet by twenty feet. I felt I had made the best possible choice.

I stood with hands on hips looking at the plot of gravel and the pile of logs beside it. The logs were decked, one layer one way and the next at right angles to it so air could circulate through the pile. On that floor of gravel, from those logs, the house would grow. I could see it before me because I had sketched it so many times. It would be eleven feet by fifteen feet on the inside. Its front door would face northwest, and the big window would look down the lake to the south and west. It would nestle there as if it belonged.

A pile of logs. Which ones to start with. Why not the largest and most crooked for the two side foundation logs? They would be partly buried in the gravel anyway. Save the best ones to show off to the best possible advantage. I rolled the logs around until I was satisfied I had found what I was looking for.

One log in particular required considerable hewing to straighten it. I must say white spruce works up nicely with axe and drawknife, much like white pine. If I keep the edges of my tools honed, it will be a pleasure to pile up chips and shavings.

I bedded the two side logs into the gravel, then selected two end logs, which I laid across them to form the eleven-by-fifteen-foot interior. Next I scribed the notches on the underside of the end logs, on each side so the entire pattern of the notch was joined and penciled. Everything inside the pencil patterns would have to be removed. Four notches to cut out.

To make a notch fit properly, you can't rush it. Make several saw cuts an inch or two apart almost down to the pencil line and whack out the chunks with the axe until the notch is roughly formed. Then comes the finish work, the careful custom fit. I have just the tool for the job. At first I thought the character in the hardware store gouged me a little when he charged more than seven dollars for a gouge chisel (half round), but next to my axe I consider it my most valuable tool. Just tap the end of its handle with the spruce mallet and the sharp edge moves a curl of wood before it, right to the line. It smooths the notch to perfection.

The four notches rolled snugly into position over the curve of the side foundation logs beneath them.

Well, there's the first course, the first four logs, and those notches couldn't fit better. That's the way they're all going to fit.

Enough for this evening. The job has begun. It should be good going from here up to the eave logs and the start of the gable ends. Tomorrow should see more working and less figuring.

I wanted a salad for supper. Fireweed greens make the best, and fireweed is one of the most common plants in this country. Its spikes of reddish pink brighten the land. They start blooming from the bottom and travel up as the season progresses. When the blossoms reach the top, summer is almost gone.

I went down along the creek bed where a dwarf variety grows. None were in bloom yet. I squatted among the stems and slender leaves and picked the tender plant crowns into a bowl. Then I rinsed them in the creek.

Sprinkled with sugar and drizzled with vinegar, those wild greens gave the red beans just the tang needed.

■ *May 26th.* I should have a fish for this evening's meal. It was a good morning to try for one down at the connecting stream.

There was still ice on the lower half of the lake. The way the ice was moving yesterday I thought the lake would be clear of it. Something is stalling the ice parade.

Traveling the lake shore, I nearly upended a time or two on the crusted snow. It was treacherous going. When I came to a good seat on the evergreens beneath a small spruce, I took advantage of it and proceeded to glass the slopes above the spruce timber.

First sighting was a cow moose with a yearling trailing her down country. While I watched them, I heard the bawling of caribou calves. It took me a few minutes to locate where all the noise was coming from. In a high basin I spotted seventy-five or more cows and calves. Across the lake ten Dall rams were in different positions of relaxation, and farther down I counted eleven lambs and nineteen ewes. Satisfied that there was plenty of game in the country, I trudged down to the stream and followed along its banks, through the hummocks of low brush, until I came to where it poured invitingly into the lower lake.

I waded out a few steps. My boots did not leak, but almost immediately the chill seeped through the woolens inside them. I cast a few times, letting the small metal lure ride out with the current, then retrieving it jerkily with twitches of the rod tip. Several more casts. Nothing.

Then it happened with the suddenness of a broken shoelace. As the lure came flashing toward me over the gravel, a pale shadow, almost invisible against the bottom, streaked in pursuit. Jaws gaped white, and the bright glint of the lure winked out as they closed over it. The line hissed, the rod tip hooped. The fish swerved out of the shallows, rolling a bulge of water before him as he bolted for the dropoff. He slashed the water white as I backed away with the rod held high, working him in to where he ran out of water and flopped his yellow spotted sides on the bank. A nineteen-inch lake trout. I thumped its head with a stone, and it shuddered out straight.

As I dressed it out, I examined its stomach. Not a thing in it. It is always interesting to see what a fish has been eating. Several times I have found mice in the stomachs of lake trout and arctic char. Now how does a mouse get himself into a jackpot like that? Does he fall in by accident, or does he venture for a swim? Tough to be a mouse in this country. From the air, the land, and the water his enemies wait to strike.

On the way back to the cabin, I repaired the log bridge over Hope Creek. All it needed was shoring up with a few boulders rolled against the log bracings on each end, which was easier to do now while the water was low.

I popped a batch of corn in bacon fat, salted and buttered it, and munched on it while I studied the sweep of the mountains. Before I left for the construction job, I shaped my biscuits, put them into a pan, and covered them to rise for supper. You always have to think ahead with biscuits and a lot of other things in the wilderness.

If I can fit eight logs a day, the cabin will go along at a good rate. That's sixteen notches to cut out and tailor to fit. It is important to put the notch on the underside of a log and fit it down over the top of the one beneath. If you notch the topside, rain will run into it instead of dripping past in a shingle effect. Water settling into the notches can cause problems.

The sun shining on the green lake ice was so beautiful I had to stop work now and then just to look at it. That's a luxury a man enjoys when he works for himself.

For supper, I cut the trout into small chunks, dipped them into beaten egg, and rolled them in cornmeal. They browned nicely in the bacon fat, and my tender crusted sourdoughs did justice to the first fish fry of the season.

■ *May 28th.* Frost on the logs when I went to work at six A.M. I had to roll many of them around to get the ones I wanted. Sorting takes time, but matching ends is very important if the cabin is to look right.

The wind helped the ice along today. The upper lake is nearly two-thirds ice-free now.

Had my first building inspector at the job. A gray jay, affectionately known as camp robber, came in his drab uniform of gray and white and black to look things over from his perch on a branch end. The way he kept tilting his head and making those mewing sounds, I'd say he was being downright critical. I welcomed his company just the same.

■ *May 29th.* Only a few chunks of ice floating in the lake this morning. By noon there was no ice to be seen. It was good to see the lake in motion again. It was even better to slip the canoe into the water and paddle to work for a change, gliding silently along over a different pathway.

My logs are not as uniform as they could be. They have too much taper, which makes much more work. Just the same I like the accumulation of white chips and shavings all over the ground and the satisfaction that comes from making a log blend over the curve of the one beneath it as if it grew that way. You can't rush it. I don't want these logs looking as though a Boy Scout was turned loose on them with a dull hatchet.

This evening I hauled out Spike's heavy trotline, tested it for strength, and baited its three hooks with some of the lake trout fins. I whirled it a few times, gave it a toss, and watched the stone sinker zip the slack line from the beach and land with a plop about fifty feet from the shore. Let's see what is prowling the bottom these days.

It was raining slightly when I turned in. There's no sleeping pill like a good day's work.

■ *May 30th.* A trace of new snow on the crags.

After breakfast I checked the trotline. It pulled heavy, with a tugging now and then on the way in. Two burbot, a fifteen-incher and a nineteen-incher. A burbot is ugly, all mottled and bigheaded—it looks like the result of an eel getting mixed up with a codfish. It tastes a whole lot better than it looks. I skinned and cleaned the two before going to work and left the entrails on the beach for the sanitation department.

The cabin is growing. Twenty-eight logs are in place. Forty-four should do it, except for gable ends and the roof logs. It really looks a mess to see the butts extending way beyond the corners, but I will trim them off later on.

Rain halted operations for a spell.

When I started in again, I made a blunder. My mind must have been on the big ram I had been watching. I'd just finished a notch, had a real dandy fit, and was about ready to fasten it down when I noticed it was wrong end to! I tossed it to one side and started another. Guess a man needs an upset now and then to remind him that he doesn't know as much as he thinks he does. Maybe that's what the camp robber was trying to tell me.

■ *May 31st.* A weird-looking country this morning. The fog last night froze on the mountains, giving them a light gray appearance. That loon calling out of the vapor sounds like the spirit of Edgar Allan Poe.

The contrary log of yesterday carried over into today. I carefully fitted and fastened it down, and was selecting logs for the next course when I looked up and saw it was still wrong end to! How in the world did that happen? Two big ends together are proper but not three. I pried it off and flung it to the side. But why get shook up about it? It's better to discover it now than when it's buried beneath a course.

Thirty-five logs in place. Nine to go and I will be ready for the gables—those tricky triangular sections on each end beneath the pitch of the roof. The roof logs and the ridge will notch over them. Babe said he could fly in some plywood for a roof. There would be room to spare in the Stinson, but plywood seems too easy. I think I will stick with the pole idea instead. Run those spruce poles at right angles to the eave logs and the ridge, then decide the best way to cover them.

It was snowing a few flakes as I worked. Cool weather is the best kind to work in, although rain makes the logs slick. Very few insects about. No complaints there.

I have a kettle of navy beans soaking for tomorrow. Babe says they must be at least fifteen years old. At that rate they will need a long bath.

■ *June 1st.* Fog lifted early. This commuting to work by canoe is the best way yet.

Just fitted the jinx log into place when I heard a plane. It was Babe. I watched the T-craft glide in for a perfect landing on the calm lake. I've heard bush pilots say it is much easier to land where there is a ripple, because calm water distorts depth perception. I shoved off in the canoe and rounded the point to meet him at Spike's beach.

Plenty of groceries this time. Fifty pounds of sugar, fifty pounds of flour, two gallons of honey, sixty pounds of spuds, two dozen eggs, half a slab of bacon, some rhubarb plants, plenty of mail, and some books . . . religious ones. I guess he has been working overtime on my philosophy from our last chat on the beach.

Babe had planted his potatoes yesterday. He was in a hurry. No time to visit. Wished he had time to inspect the building project. Next time he would. Right now he had a couple of prospectors to fly in somewhere. He would see me in a couple of weeks.

I got mail from all over. Brother Jake is flying up and down that California country. Wish I could talk him into coming up here and staying a spell. We'd see some sights in that little bird of his.

Sister Florence is going to make a set of curtains for my big window. Dad is fine but he wishes I had a large dog with me. I've thought about a dog. It would mess up my picture-taking for sure.

Sid Old is still soaking up the sun in New Mexico. The old boy has been off his feed lately. I could listen to him all day, spinning his yarns about the early horse-packing days on Kodiak: tying the diamond hitch, the cattle-killing bears.

Spike allows that he and Hope may drop in to Twin Lakes in August. Spike not quite up to snuff these days either. Sam Keith writes that the kids in the junior high school where he is vice principal are like beef critters smelling water after a long drive. They smell vacation. Wish I could get him up here with that willow wand of his when the grayling are having an orgy at the creek mouth. Good to hear from everybody. I guess part of a man's root system has to be nourished by contacts with family and old friends.

The rhubarb plants should be put into the ground right away. Why not plant the whole garden patch while I'm at it?

I found the frost about four or five inches down. I drove the grub hoe into the soil as far as I could and stirred up the plot with a shallow spading. The loam seemed quite light and full of humus. I set out the rhubarb plants and watered them. Then I planted fifteen hills of potatoes, tucked in some onion sets, and sowed short rows of peas, carrots, beets, and rutabagas. Not much of a garden by Iowa standards, but it would tell me what I wanted to find out.

Finally back to the cabin building. I'm a better builder than I am a farmer anyway. Thirty-eight logs are in place and I'm almost ready for the eave logs.

Where are the camp robbers and the spruce squirrel? I miss seeing them. They are good companions, but work is really the best one of all.

A fine evening and I hated to waste it. The lake was flat calm and a joy to travel with quiet strokes of the paddle. My excuse was to prospect for some roof-pole timber near Whitefish Point. I found no great amount, and I returned to this side of the lake.

■ *June 3rd.* I am ready for the eave logs and the gables. I marked out the windows and door and will cut far enough into each log so that once the eave logs are on, I can get the saw back through to finish the cutting.

The gables and the roof have occupied much of my thoughts lately. Up to this point my line level tells me the sides and ends are on the money. The course logs were selected carefully, and I have done the hewing necessary to keep the opposite sides level as the cabin grows. Five logs were very special. These were the twenty-footers, which along with the gable ends would be the backbone of the roof. Two would be eave logs, two purlin logs, and the last, the straightest, would be the ridge log. In pondering how to go about the gables, I pictured to myself the letter A. It would take four logs, one atop the other and each one shorter than the one beneath, to make a triangle up to the ridge log height I planned.

The eave logs are the top ones on the side walls. They would be different from the other wall logs in that they would overhang about a foot in the rear of the cabin and extend three feet beyond the front of the cabin, to hold the eaves and the porch roof. The purlin logs are roof beams running parallel with the length of the cabin, halfway between the eave logs and the ridge log. The roof poles would lie over them at right angles, from the ridge down across the eave logs.

Of course the ridge log still was not in place. To get it there, the fourth and shortest gable log would be spiked on top of the third one. The ridge would be seated on it, equally spaced between the purlins. There would be a framework of five logs, two (or eaves) at the top of the walls, one (the ridge) at the peak, and two (the purlins) in between, supporting the crossways roof poles.

The gable ends will be cut to the slope of the roof. The slope can be determined with a chalk line. I'll drive a nail on top of the ridge pole, draw the string down along the face of the gable logs, just over the top of the purlins, to the eave nails. I'll chalk the line, pull it tight, and snap it. The blue chalk lines slanting down the gable logs will represent the slope of the roof on each side. The gable logs then can be cut at the proper angle of the letter A I've pictured.

The three-foot extension of the roof logs in front of the cabin will allow for three feet of shed-like entrance to the cabin.

That's the way the project shapes up. Let's see if we can do it.

■ *June 4th.* A good day to start the roof skeleton.

Another critic cruised past in the lake this morning, a real chip expert and wilderness engineer, Mr. Beaver. He probably got a little jealous of all the chips he saw, and to show what he thought of the whole deal, upended and spanked his tail on the surface before he disappeared.

Shortly afterward a pair of harlequin ducks came by for a look. The drake is handsome with those white splashes against gray and rusty patches of cinnamon.

My curiosity got the better of me and I had to glass the sheep in the high pasture. It was a sight to watch the moulting ewes grazing as the lambs frolicked about, jumping from a small rock and bounding over the greenery, bumping heads. It was a happy interruption to my work.

I find I can handle the twenty-footers easily enough by just lifting one end at a time. With the corners of the cabin not yet squared off, there are some long ends sticking out on which to rest logs as I muscle them up to eave level and beyond. I also have two logs leaning on end within the cabin, and by adjusting their tilt I can use them to position a log once it is up there. The ladder comes in handy, too.

The two eave logs were notched and fastened down according to plan. I cut the openings for the big window, the two smaller ones, and the opening for the door. I placed the first gable log on each end, and it was time to call it a day.

The roof skeleton should get the rest of its bones tomorrow.

■ *June 5th.* Good progress today. When you first think something through, you have a pretty good idea where you are going and eliminate a lot of mistakes.

I put up the gable ends, notched the purlin logs into them, and fastened down the ridge log. It went smoothly. It's a good thing I put the eave log one row higher than I had originally planned, or I would have to dig out for headroom. Even now a six-footer won't have any to spare, and I won't have much more clearance myself.

The cabin is in a good spot. That up-the-lake wind is blocked by the timber and brush between the cabin and the mouth of Hope Creek.

As it now stands, the cabin looks as though logs are sticking out all over it like the quills of a riled porcupine. There's much trimming to do in the morning. All logs are plenty long, so there will be no short ones to worry about.

■ *June 6th.* The time has come to cut the cabin down to size. First I filed the big saw. Then I trimmed the roof logs to the proper length. I trimmed the gable logs to the slope of the roof, and trimmed the wall logs on all four corners. What a difference! Log ends are all over the ground and the cabin is looking like a once-shaggy kid after a crew cut.

Now I have to start thinking about window and door frames, and the roof poles. I must find a stand of skinny timber for those. That means some prospecting in the standing lumberyards.

My cabin logs have magically changed form in the ten days since I cut the first notch. There are only four full-length logs left, and only one of those is halfway decent. Before it's over, there will be a use for all of them.

■ *June 7th.* I do believe the growing season is at hand. The buckbrush and willows are leafing out fast now. The rhubarb is growing, and I notice my onion sets are spiking up through the earth.

Those window frames have been on my mind. I decided to do something about it. First I built a sawhorse workbench, then selected straight-grained sections of logs cut from the window and door openings. I chalked a line down each side, and with a thin-bladed wide chisel, I cut deep along the line on each side. Then I drove the hand axe into the end to split the board away from the log. That worked fine.

I smoothed the split sides with the drawknife to one and three-quarter inches wide. The result was a real nice board, so I continued to fashion others. Put in place and nailed, they look first-rate.

I finished the day cleaning the litter of wood chips. I mounded them in front of the door, beaver lodge style. Quite a pile for eleven days' work— enough to impress that beaver.

I have given a lot of thought to chinking. I think I will try mixing moss and loose oakum to cut down on the amount of oakum. If oakum with its hemp fibers can caulk the seams in boats, it should be able to chink logs.

■ *June 8th.* I moved my mountain of wood chips and shavings. Then I gathered moss and spread it on the beach to dry. There is still ice under the six-inch-thick moss in the woods. I used oakum in the narrow seams, and a mixture of oakum and moss where the opening was more than one-quarter inch. Straight oakum is easier to use. I will have a tight cabin.

■ *June 9th.* Today would be a day away from the job of building. I'll look for pole timber up the lake.

I proceeded to the upper end of the lake, where I beached the canoe on the gravel bar and tied the painter to a willow clump. A "down-the-lake" wind might come up and work the canoe into the water, and it would be a long hike to retrieve it.

I walked along the flat, crossing and recrossing the creek that had its beginnings in the far-off snows. I found a dropped moose antler, a big one, and decided to pick it up on the way back. There were fox tracks and lynx tracks in the sand, and piles of old moose droppings.

The rockpile was finally before me, a huge jumble of gray-black, sharp-edged granite chunks all crusted with lichens. It was a natural lookout that commanded three canyons. I set up my spotting scope, wedging the legs of the tripod firmly amid the slim-fronded ferns that grew dagger-shaped in single clumps out of the rock crevices. Right off I spotted four caribou bulls grazing along the right fork of the creek bed. Then high on the slopes five good-looking

Dall rams, one in a classic pose with all four feet together atop a crag, back humped against the sky.

Below them, four ewes moved in my direction. At mid-slope a bull moose on the edge of some cottonwoods was pulling at the willow brush, changing black and brown as he swung his antlers among the foliage. I saw an eagle wheeling in the air currents, pinions stiffened like outstretched fingers. Ground squirrels whistled. Life was all around.

On the way back to the beach I stooped to nibble on last season's moss-berries. They were a little tart to the tongue. I picked up the moose antler and wondered where the other might be. To my surprise I found the mate not 200 yards away. They made quite an awkward load to pack. It must be a relief to an old bull when the load falls off.

Just as I reached the canoe, it had to happen. An up-the-lake-wind! I battled against it for a spell, then decided to beach. Finding a warm spot in the sun I napped, waiting for the lake to flatten. It never really did, and I paddled back from point to point until I finally reached the cabin.

A good day. I forgot only one thing—something for lunch.

▪ *June 10th.* Bright and clear. I hear the spruce squirrel, but he stays out of sight. He likes to shuck his spruce cones in private. The blueberry bushes are nearly leafed out and loaded with bloom.

I finished chinking the cabin. Then I put a log under the bottom log in front, to plug an opening there. I did the same in back and chinked them both. Now I am ready for the roof poles, which I will start cutting tomorrow.

The little sandpipers flying back and forth along the edge of the beach have a characteristic flight. A few quivering strokes of their wings, a brief sail, some more wing vibrations, and then wings rigid again as they glide to a landing and vanish. They blend in so well, they are invisible against the gravel until they move.

▪ *June 11th.* I paddled up the lake to the foot of Crag Mountain. This was a pole-cutting day.

Good poles were not as plentiful as I figured, and I worked steadily to get forty-eight cut and packed to the beach by noon. The mosquitoes were out in force.

To peel the poles, I made a tripod of short sticks on which to rest one end of the pole while the other stuck into the bank, and put the drawknife to work. The bark flew.

▪ *June 12th.* Today I finished peeling the poles, fifty in all, rafted them up, and moved them down the lake to my beach. A good pile, but I doubt there will be enough.

▪ *June 13th.* Rain. Wrote a batch of letters—not a job to do on a good day. It cleared in the late afternoon, so I gathered sixteen more poles and peeled seven.

▪ *June 14th.* Not a cloud in the sky. A cool morning but no frost. My garden is all up except the potatoes, and they should be showing soon. The green onions are more than three inches tall.

I peeled the remainder of my roof poles and trimmed the knots close. Now to put them on, but how close? I decided on five inches center to center as they lay at right angles to the ridge log.

One side is nearly roofed and the other, about half. With only ten left, I must hunt more poles—about thirty if my calculations are right.

▪ *June 15th.* I tried for a fish this morning at the mouth of Hope Creek. No luck. I did see the flash of a light-colored belly behind the lure. They are there.

I went pole prospecting below the creek mouth in the fine rain and cut fifteen—enough for one trip back up the lake. I tied the small ends side by side, ran the canoe into the butt-ends far enough to tie them to the bow thwart. It left me enough room to paddle from just forward of the stern, which worked real well—slow but effective transportation.

In the afternoon I finished the front end of the cabin roof and took count. I would need seventeen more poles. After scouting in the timber behind the cabin, I found seven.

A beautiful evening with a light breeze down the lake. A loon rode low in the water and trailed a wake of silver as it took flight.

■ *June 16th.* Where are my spuds? Maybe I planted them too deep.

Today I secured the roof poles over the gables and chinked them. A cabin roof takes time. A hundred poles to gather, transport, and peel, trim the knots, and notch them to fit over the purlin logs. I see where one more pole is needed. Soon I will be ready to saw the ends and fill the slots between the pole butts under the eaves. These fillers should be called squirrel frustrators. Give those characters an entrance and they can ruin a cabin.

■ *June 17th.* Up to greet the new day at 3:45 A.M. I am not sure of the time anymore. I have kept both my watch and clock wound but have not changed the setting. Now they are thirty minutes apart. Which one is right? No radio to check by. I don't miss a radio a bit. I never thought one was in tune with the wilderness anyway. A man is on his own frequency out here.

On the job at five-thirty. I sawed the roof pole ends off to a proper eighteen-inch overhang. Now I am ready for the chore of plugging the gaps between the roof poles on top of the wall logs. If varmints are going to get into my cabin, they will have to work at it.

The camp robbers are back. Four were near the cabin today. They are marked somewhat like king-size chickadees. I like the way they come gliding softly in to settle on a spruce tip and tilt their heads from one side to the other as if they are critical of what I am doing. Some have a very dark plumage, almost black.

Tomorrow should see the roof ready for the tar paper, polyethylene, and moss. I feel guilty about the tar paper and polyethylene because they are not true wilderness cabin materials, but I am convinced that they will do a better job of keeping the weather out. Next I will finish the inside kitchen counter, table, and bench and make stands for the water bucket and the wash basin. The more I think about it, I should build a double-deck bunk. Might have some company.

■ *June 18th.* Everything looks as though it had a bath last night. Must have been a good shower and I never even heard it.

My garden looks perky. The green onions are five inches tall or more. Peas are up an inch. Everything is growing first-class but my spuds. Not a sign of them yet.

A check on the livestock before going down to the roof job. Two caribou bulls just up country from Low Pass Creek. Nothing else in sight. Should be a bear passing through one of these days.

I finished filling the slots between the roof poles and caulked joints with oakum. Then I put a strip of the oiled oakum down each side and over the gables. I chinked around the blocks on the outside and also caught the windows and door frame. I chinked all the corner joints of the logs. Any place I could get a table knife blade in got oakum.

I was surprised to look up and see it raining on the other side of the lake. It was darkening fast. The rain was advancing on the double. A get-wet rain was upon me before I made it to Spike's cabin. Six o'clock by the Baby Ben. Time for the sourdough biscuits and those red beans.

Once I get my roof on, I can work on the cabin rain or shine.

I do believe this rain will help the blueberry crop. Seems to me there are more blossoms than last summer.

Twenty days to get the cabin to its present stage of construction. A lot of chips ago.

■ *June 19th.* I need a fish. No luck at all at Hope Creek. I decided to paddle down to the upper end of the lower lake. There ought to be some action where the connecting stream pours in.

It took an hour and ten minutes to make the run on the calm water. Then instant action. I took two seventeen-inch lake trout out of the eddies near the fast water. That's enough for my needs, so I packed up and lined the canoe against the current to the upper lake. I saw a sharply defined wolf track in the mud. Next time down I must try a plaster cast of that.

In the afternoon while checking the country through the spotting scope, I gasped right out loud. I saw caribou all over the place! I couldn't pass this up, so I loaded the canoe with my camera gear and the plaster of paris. These cows and calves were just beyond where the big wolf track was. I made record time down to the lower end of the lake.

First things first. I prepared the wolf track. It should be ready by the time I get back from stalking the caribou. The mud was very wet and I wondered if the plaster would set, but I filled the track up anyway with the thick mixture.

As I climbed through the timber, the herd started to move down country. There were at least 150. The breeze was in my favor, with plenty of cover to get close. I never saw so many caribou in the viewfinder at one time. There they were, bedded down in that wild setting, and when they started to move suddenly, the whole land seemed to move with them. I should have some good footage from that show. On the way back to the canoe I looked back and there were the tail-enders trailing up through the pass.

The plaster had not set up in the track. It was as soft as when I had put it down. I cut a piece of cardboard from a box I had in the canoe, for a base. I cut around the track and the plaster, pushed my fingers under from opposite sides, lifted up, and set the whole blob like a cake onto the cardboard.

A breezy tailwind helped me paddle home.

More good luck. The trotline pulled heavy. A twenty-inch burbot. I'm back in the fish business.

■ *June 20th.* A fog barrier hid the peaks.

There's more chinking to do around the filler blocks and the roof poles, around the purlin logs where they go through the gables, and at the corner joints on the inside as well as the outside.

Next was a job I had been thinking about, a table top, a counter top, some window ledges, and some shelves. I could split the logs straight enough but there were many slivers, and it was a real chore to get them halfway smooth. I made two, then decided to try ripping one with the ripsaw. That was the answer. I could go down the middle of a log five inches in diameter and forty-two inches long in fifteen minutes. Couldn't complain about that.

I think I have sawed nearly everything that I need. Now to trim the edges and start building.

A few rain showers forced me to get the sixteen-foot by ten-foot tarp of polyethylene, and I covered the overhang in front of the cabin with it. A dry place to work, and my tools will keep as well.

What about that! One of my spuds has appeared!

■ *June 21st.* A big surprise this morning. A white frost and a good one. The leaves of the rhubarb were white. I wondered how my garden would fare with this sneak attack. When the sun started bearing down, I would know.

I was sitting in my doorway filing the teeth of the ripsaw. When I looked up for a moment, I noticed a movement on the gravel path leading up from the lake. At first glance I thought it was the squirrel, but the movements were even more furtive and the animal was too skinny to be a squirrel. Surely enough, it was a weasel. He stopped within six feet of me. His eyes held the glint of black beads as they peered at me out of a triangular-shaped head. His ears were rounded. He was wearing his summer coat of pale brown with white undertrimmings. His tail was black from the tip right on up to the middle of it.

My hand moved to brush at a gnat crawling on my eyelid. In a flash the weasel was off, scampering over the hummocks of moss.

The squirrel chattered from the very top of a spruce. There he was against the sky, sitting on his haunches, tail curved over his back, nibbling on a spruce cone that he held in his forepaws. The scales were raining down on the boughs below him.

"Quiet up there," I warned. "You better watch out. That bloodthirsty guy will have you for breakfast."

A day to make lumber. Hew off the round side of my slabs and trim the edges. I ripped out two planks for my door, and will need two more. Soon I will be ready to put things together.

The frost seems not to have hurt the garden one bit but something else almost did. Fresh moose tracks that just missed. I hope the frost didn't bother the blueberries.

■ *June 22nd.* Got up before the sun and watched it light the peaks of the shadowed mountains.

The sound of a plane. In came Babe, landing downwind. I saw his boy, Glenn, climb out on the pilot's side. That little fellow in the eighth grade next year was flying the old T-craft!

They'd brought lots of groceries—rhubarb and oranges and grapefruit and bananas—and mail. Some spikes and two goodhand saws. Also a cake from Mary Alsworth.

Babe was satisfied the cabin was coming along fine. We sat on the beach for a spell. He would be using the old Stinson to ferry gas for a prospecting outfit. Did I want anything big flown in? Could I use a fifty-gallon barrel or two? Good to store stuff in, so the varmints can't get at it. I allowed they might come in handy.

I watched them go out of sight over the volcanic mountains.

I got some really sad news in my mail. Senator Robert Kennedy was assassinated.

I must admit Mary Alsworth bakes a better cake than I do.

■ *June 23rd.* Sunday. A day to take up the slack.

Saws to sharpen. That's an easy job. Then a hunt for a log to make some two-inch planks for my cabin door. I found one in my wood supply. It would make two planks nine inches wide. With the two I already had, that should give me enough. I marked out the planks. It would take some ripping to make three cuts fifty-one inches long and ten deep. But I went at it and in time the job was done. I could use the slabs for bench tops or stool tops, or whatever. I loaded the whole business into the canoe and paddled down to the cabin.

Fog wisps around the peaks, and a sprinkle dimples the calm lake this evening.

■ *June 24th.* A dusting of new snow on Spike's Peak.

A few more boards to hew out and then I will start on the inside. Window ledges for three windows. A five-foot shelf over the door and the start of the kitchen counter cut out and ready to put on the wall. I augered one-and-a-half-inch holes into the wall logs to take the supports for the counter. There will be no legs on the floor. Tomorrow I will do what I can toward the construction of the table, make the door, and then the double-deck bunk.

More spuds waking up.

A strong breeze is coming down the lake this evening. Best repellent I know; it keeps the mosquitoes grounded.

■ *June 25th.* Sunlight on the slopes down country. A beautiful day.

Put some finishing touches on the door planks I made Sunday. Now the door is ready to put together. I think I shall make it a Dutch door. I made the legs for a table. All I have to do is auger four holes and it will be ready to assemble. Installed three window ledges and cut the window sash to fit the frames. I installed half the kitchen counter framework. Made and put up three shelves in the kitchen area. Tomorrow I will work on my double-deck bunk. To look around at what you have accomplished in a day gives a man a good feeling. Too many men work on parts of things. Doing a job to completeness satisfies a man.

■ *June 26th.* A cool morning. My garden is like a turtle with its head pulled in. It needs the warm sun to respond.

Today I built the double bunk. Four posts with two rails on each side, and two large and two small rails on each end. I augered one-and-a-half-inch holes and trimmed the rail poles to fit. I got it put together and it looked too big so I shortened the end rails. Still too big, so I cut them again. I have it down now to twenty-seven inches wide inside the side rails, and it looks much better. Now when I get some glue, I will knock it apart and glue it back together.

Tomorrow I will set the legs for my table and build a stool and a bench.

Thundering down country. The lake is going down, and the waterfall across the lake isn't running its usual amount. Twin Lakes needs a good rain.

■ *June 27th.* A good rain it was. My garden looks rejuvenated.

Today will be a pole-hunting day. I need about thirty to make the slats for my bunks, small but of good length, which is a tough combination. I will have to investigate the Twin Lakes Lumberyard pretty thoroughly.

I paddled down country and struck it rich. I found a spruce thicket such as I have never seen in this country: saplings an inch or a bit over at the butt and ten feet tall—just what I needed. I had them cut in no time. Loaded them into the canoe and paddled across the puddle-still lake to home.

While I was peeling the poles the wind came up strong from an unusual quarter—directly across from Allen Mountain. It brought rain and it furrowed the lake as rough as a cob. This lake can really change its personality in a hurry. Like a woman all smiles one minute and dancing a temper tantrum the next. I was happy to find I had enough bunk poles and even some extras that I could use for stool and bench logs.

The wind died as abruptly as it came. Now the lake is grinning with reflections again. A picture evening.

■ *June 28th.* Bright as crystal this morning and not a cloud to be seen.

A furniture building day. First a kitchen chair and then a bench three feet long. The echoing of the axe, the whacking noises of the driven chisel, the crisp bite of the sharp auger into wood, the gathering pile of chips and shavings—and both articles ready to glue before noon.

I weeded my garden at lunch time and watered it. The peas are looking healthy and the green onions are almost ready to use.

I am near the end of the building job on the cabin until Babe comes. He's supposed to bring glue and the polyethylene for my roof.

I spent the afternoon cleaning up scraps. The wild roses are blooming in the cabin yard. The ground dogwood and the little moss flowers are out. And people spend money for lawn mowers and waste time walking behind them!

I finally got around to sharpening my tools as I do every evening. Time to call it a day. A gentle breeze was moving up the lake as I trudged the beach to Spike's cabin and supper.

■ *June 29th.* The growing season is definitely at hand. The blueberry blossoms are starting to fall, and soon I will have to check on the young berries.

Today's thought was to put hinges on my windows. I need a three-legged stool and a book-rack type of shelf to store books, camera gear, and clothes. This last project would take some doing as it would require three shelves three feet long, ranging from fifteen to twelve inches in width. Lots of ripping to turn out that much lumber.

The job was done, with a good-feeling right arm to prove it. The rustic rack has a lonesome look. It needs filling. That will come soon enough.

I thought for a spell about a roof-jack to take the stovepipe. That is important. A man thinks better when he's working. Beneath the thirty-five inch overhang in front of the cabin I augered holes into the logs and drove in pegs, good hanging places for stuff better off outside than in. I'm still figuring about that jack.

Tomorrow is Sunday. I will go someplace.

■ *June 30th.* A third of the way down to Emerson Creek, the wind blew strong in my face and it was a real battle to keep headway in the chop of the water. I had my knees spread wide against the canoe bottom, and I had to put back and shoulders into the job to make the creek. Those sourdough pancakes must have a high octane content. I had come down to prospect for suitable stumps from which to fashion wooden hinges. Steel hinges are better, no doubt, but it is interesting to see what one can do using only material from the forest.

While foraging among the uprooted trees, I noticed wolf tracks mixed in with the caribou tracks, and I thought of my plaster cast. I would have to check that out. I couldn't find the hinge stock I wanted. The trees were too big. I would have to try another department of the lumberyard another time.

What I did find, though, on the trek back along the creek bed to the canoe, was a squarish, pale orange rock. I have a feeling it will be the center rock in the arch of the fireplace.

I noticed the boss hunter's plane came in today. He didn't stay long at his cabin, just long enough to check his camp for supplies he would need when he brought in the trophy boys during the sheep season. I wonder if the big rams feel that first stir of uneasiness? Do they know the difference between his plane and Babe's?

The wind I fought before, now helped me home. Wind and fire. Help you one minute and kill you the next. All depends on the time and place.

■ *July 1st.* This morning I fashioned a box for the plaster cast of the wolf track. I sawed off the end of a cabin log and made a two-and-a-quarter-inch slice for the box, and a one-and-three-quarter-inch slice for the lid. I hollowed them out with the wood auger and chisel and now have a neat box. I will mix some plaster, pour it in, then bed my cast in it and let it set.

That roof-jack for the stove pipe, I've been thinking about. Select the proper location, and nail a cross tie to support the two roof poles. Reinforce the base of the roof-jack to make it wider and stiffer. The pipe will be installed so it will stay there without wires. A few sheet metal screws should do it.

Time to put the tar paper over the roof poles and fasten it down. Not forest material but I had better use it.

Later: The tar paper project is off. Heavy rain—a good soaking, one to replenish the forest sponge.

A problem. How to clean the million tiny chips and grains of sawdust out of the gravel on the cabin floor? An idea. Pack all the gravel back out and toss it into the lake. The chips and dust stayed on the surface and drifted away. I shoveled the gravel back on the beach, let it drain, and packed it back again. Clean wall-to-wall gravel once more.

■ *July 2nd.* The lake is like a sheet of glass.

My roof poles are too wet for the tar paper. This gives me a chance to go prospecting again for some hinge timber. I figure I need the butt end of eight small trees to make four sets of hinges.

A peaceful trip down the lake gliding through the reflections of the mountains. After scouting around, I located ten seasoned spruce stump sections. Took a few extra in case I had a bad one or made a wrong cut. A few unusual looking rocks found their way into the canoe also.

I had a good load. This was a chance to see the difference in traveling time between a loaded canoe and an empty one. One hour to the minute to my cabin site from the lower end. I doubt if I have ever beaten that time, running empty.

Just as I beached the canoe, I saw ruffled water not far behind. The breeze brought rain.

I was anxious to try making hinges. I saw a cabin once with some, but they were very crude. I worked the wood to shape with axe and drawknife. Now to saw the fork in the butt end. Forty-five minutes and I had half my hinge made. Not bad.

It was still raining when I came back from a lunch of sourdough pancake sandwiches of peanut butter and last summer's blueberry jelly.

Another tree made the other half of the hinge, and the next tree made a complete hinge. Two more to go, and the hinges will be ready to auger holes for their pins. The hinges will serve another purpose. They are long enough to serve as battens for holding the door planks together.

It started to rain hard. While I waited the shower out, I honed my cutting tools to real fine edges.

I checked the garden. The peas are grabbing hold of the brush supports I stuck along the row the other day.

■ *July 3rd.* A cool, damp morning with fog coming off the slope like the smoke from many campfires.

I finished my hinges. All they need now is the holes augered for the pins. I can do that another time. No wind now, so it is perfect for the tar-paper job.

I lapped the tarred felt paper four to five inches. I need just one more strip twenty feet long. There's another roll in Spike's cabin. I must admit the cabin looks better already with the start of a roof.

Tomorrow is the Fourth. I should take a trip, but Babe might pick the holiday to fly in. I had better stick close to camp.

■ *July 4th.* A big stack of sourdoughs this morning. Hope Babe does come. I'm about out of bacon and eggs, but I can do without.

I got a twelve-inch arctic char on the trotline. It will be the main attraction for lunch. A char, with a more satiny sheen than a lake trout, is a cousin of the brook trout.

I finished the tar-paper job on the roof first thing. If I only had the poly-ethylene, I could have it all ready for the moss chunks cut from the forest floor.

I worked some more on the hinges, augered the holes to take the seven-eighth-inch hinge pins of spruce. I am anxious to see how the door will look and operate with this forest hardware.

No sign of Babe. Best to keep busy. I need a woodshed so I sketched a plan of it. Twelve feet by eight feet with the toilet on one end. I would build it on the order of a log shelter, open in front, a gable with only a narrow roof over the open front to keep rain and snow from blowing in. I could set my sawbuck under the overhang.

Cleared brush for the woodshed project. I would have to cut some logs, maybe twelve or so.

Whitecaps raced along beside me as I paddled back to supper. No lives lost at Twin Lakes this holiday. I wonder how many died in the south 48?

■ *July 5th.* Clear and cold. My first thought was the spuds. There was frost on the leaves. I was sure they would turn black as soon as the sun warmed them.

No plane and no roof covering. Might as well start on the woodshed and toilet. I was surprised to find ice just under the moss. Moss is certainly a wonderful insulation.

I cut, hauled, and peeled eleven logs by noon. The sound of a plane interrupted me. It was the boss hunter coming up the lake. Was he bringing a party in this early, or was it just supplies to store and make a few repairs?

The mosquitoes gave me a bad time after lunch as I worked on the shed. Tomorrow I will use the headnet. It is really the best protection and not too bad to wear after an hour or so.

My potato leaves have just a touch of brown.

■ *July 6th.* Where are the grayling at the mouth of Hope Creek? Not a strike this morning.

Back to the woodshed project. Hewing and notching logs most of the day. I am now six logs high. I wore the headnet and had less trouble with the insects except for one getting inside now and then and wanting out, and bouncing around in front of my eyes until I had to mash it. I wore two shirts, one with no sleeves, like a vest. Even so, when I bent over, the mosquitoes would work on my back with their sharp needles. Come September I will be rid of them.

No Babe yet. He must be busy.

■ *July 7th.* An odds-and-ends day.

I put out a good-sized laundry to flutter and snap in a warm wind. Did some mending. Wrote letters and tossed them into the pile ready to go out on Babe's express. Then a visit to the Twin Lakes' barbershop. That little Penn's Easy Trim is the best investment I have made for a long time.

I went to my empty gas-can supply and spent the afternoon tin bending. I turned out a dishpan, a wash pan, eating pans, and a shelf to put above my bunk for toilet articles.

I started to read a book that Babe had brought last time. Strange how the Bible has predicted so many things that have come to pass. And now the end is near, it says. I hope I have time to finish my cabin.

■ *July 8th.* Awoke at three. I could hear rain on the sod roof, and the sky faucets really have to be wide open to do that.

Blue sky by five o'clock. The weather changes like a man's fortunes.

I would build my woodshed four feet high in back, slope the roof to an overall seven feet, then down to six feet on the short side. I found the timber I needed, dropped it, limbed it, packed it in, and peeled it. All set for material now except for roof poles.

Caught a grayling and a lake trout in the fast water rushing into the lake from Hope Creek. I didn't give them much time to carry on. The belly dictates how sporting a man is going to be.

■ *July 9th.* On the job at six. Made good progress on the gable logs, and finally set the ridge log into place. Trimmed the gables smooth from the ridge log to the eave log.

Need about thirty roof poles.

I paddled across the still lake and followed the shoreline down beyond Glacier Creek. As I glided along, I studied the cottonwood and willow belt just above the spruce timber and saw a bull moose looming black and huge out of the willow scrub. He was big and distinctive, one to watch for again.

When I beached the canoe and prowled along the bed of Glacier Creek, I found two of the whitest and roundest boulders I have ever seen.

They weighed between thirty and forty pounds each. There were others, some smaller and some bigger, but these two were mates and more perfect than all the rest. I had just the place for them. I packed them back to the canoe, loaded them gently into the bow, and paddled home. They set off the lakeshore entrance of my gravel path just right, one on either side of it. I will call them "The Grizzly Eggs."

■ _July 10th._ I had the woodshed logs gathered on the beach when I heard the plane. Babe at last! I left the poles high and dry and started the long paddle to the cabin. I met Babe walking down the beach. As usual he was in a hurry. I hoped I hadn't held him up.

Four dozen eggs this trip, a full slab of bacon, some candy bars, a big heavy Stanley jackplane dull and rusty as sin, but I could put it into shape and make the wood ribbons fly. No polyethylene. Babe said he might return later in the evening on the way back from a trip he had to make. I gave him the outgoing mail anyway, and off he went. A seventeen-and-a-half-inch lake trout on the trotline. Enough for company. Babe didn't come back.

■ _July 11th._ Calm. Perfect water for hauling my roof poles.

On the way back to the cabin site with the heavily loaded canoe, it started to rain. I beached the canoe well up on solid ground. It was nice to have the tar-paper roof overhead. While the rain pattered, I sharpened the blade of the jack-plane and oiled it. Then I moved my log bench under the overhang and proceeded to make shavings. All the boards I had ripped for shelves, counter, and table had to be planed on both sides and the two edges. Also the two-inch planks for the door. By the time I had finished, more shavings were piled up than I had ever made in a day before. I fitted the boards under the counter. The table will be ready to put together as soon as the glue arrives.

A light rain all afternoon. The mountains must be dry because there is no sign of running water yet.

A special treat for supper. I pulled some of my green onions to spice up the salad of fireweed greens.

■ _July 12th._ Heavy fog. No danger of frost today.

I put on the door hinges, first the top hinge, then a plumb bob from its center to the bottom one. I think they are positioned about right. I cut the door planks to length and ripped the last one to make the width right. I sawed out and planed the door-stop molding.

Streams are beginning to show on the mountain slopes. The lake is rising.

I fear the blueberries really took a nipping with the heavy frost not so long ago. I find some berries big and healthy, but many are small and shriveled. Looks like a shortage of blueberry pies this August and September.

▪ *July 13th.* About a dozen scoter ducks were bobbing on the rough lake this morning.

A small char on the trotline. In its stomach I found a hook I lost a few weeks back. Bright as silver, it looked better than when it was lost.

I put the roof poles on the woodshed. Next comes the indoor plumbing project. The front framework is in place, just the right height for comfort.

Sourdough biscuits drenched with navy bean soup for supper. There's a dish fit for any working man.

▪ *July 14th.* Still beset with a siege of damp weather. This will be a day for inside chores. Fire up the smoker and give that big slab of bacon some more smoke. Letters to write. Work on the wolf track box. Put on a fresh kettle of navy beans to simmer the day away.

In the afternoon I popped some corn. I accomplished what I had set out to do. A man needs a catch-up day now and then.

▪ *July 15th.* Still damp, with fog hanging low on the mountains.

Spent the day on the construction of the john, an important consideration in any new home. I made it big enough so that I could store a half-dozen empty gas cans. Materials to finish the front required lots of time ripping boards from the last of my cabin logs.

▪ *July 16th.* The sun might burn through the fog today.

My day's work cut out for me. Build the front facing for the john. Smooth all the boards with the big jack plane. Then the door: sixty-four inches high and twenty-five inches wide and not a board in the house. It will take some ripping to put out better than ten board feet.

I had a log spotted in my firewood supply, for five boards an inch thick with two slabs left over. It was twelve o'clock when I finished the last cut. Four boards would make the door and the other one, cleats to hold it together.

After lunch I trimmed the edges and planed the boards smooth. And there it was—my door. About five hours and a bit more from the log to the finished product. Probably a thirty-dollar job at Alaskan wages. I made the hinges from a gas can, three of them three and three-quarter inches wide, and they look almost store-bought. And then the final touch—saw out the crescent—and the john door was ready to hang.

■ *July 17th.* Made the partition of poles between the john and the woodshed. The chamber is now ready for serious meditation.

A tragedy! Notches in my peas, and some nipped off just above the ground. Three rows of them. I'll bet that snowshoe rabbit that hopped by the door the other day is the varmint. Probably never tasted peas before in his life. That's all I need around here—a gourmet rabbit.

■ *July 18th.* High clouds moving fast from the south.

Fresh tracks of caribou and five-inch wolf tracks in the gravel not fifty feet from my new cabin. Now wouldn't that have been a sight?

I built a stove stand and a solid sawbuck while big cotton clouds formed down country.

The droning of a plane—Babe! In he came, to make the first landing at my beach. I helped him back the tail end of the floats to rest on a spruce pole laid along the gravel. Then we tied her fast with a line.

The glue from brother Jake. That spelled progress. Plenty of mail. Still no polyethylene. Well, I'll just wait it out. Maybe next time it will come.

Babe spotted my peas. His eyes twinkled. "I like rabbit better than peas anyway," he said. "Don't you?" He helped me finish the company dessert, a can of fruit cocktail. Then he was off for Lake Clark.

I spent the rest of the day reading mail and gluing boards and poles. I do believe the cabin is close to livable.

That rabbit really likes peas. He has a rough time of it in the winter, what with lynxes and fox ready to waylay him. I really don't need the peas. Let him have them.

■ *July 19th.* Today started in a very ordinary way, yet it was to be an extraordinary one.

I canoed down to the cabin. It was a good feeling to slide into my beach. I mounted the brackets for the kitchen counter and was just putting the finishing touches on a chair when I heard an unfamiliar sound. I listened and heard it again. Then I really came to life. The sound could be only one thing—wolves howling! They were on the hump. A low deep howl again and then one higher in pitch. The chair would have to wait. I took off up the trail toward my cabin log grove. I should be able to see them from there.

Surely enough, I saw two wolves in an easy lope coming down the trail off the hump and through the scattering of small spruce. Suddenly they vanished. I froze and waited. There they were again, going back up the trail, now walking, now breaking into a slow trot.

Why didn't I bring my scope? I decided to go back and get it. I flew through heavy brush and timber and had the scope all mounted before they were halfway up the hump. It was a sight: the big one light with dark streaks on his back and sides, dark around his muzzle, the other a fourth smaller and light in shade. They traveled with tails down, long, lanky, and loose with the fur bouncing on their backs. Then there were three—another big one appeared. They stopped to smell a squirrel burrow, and as they did, their tails lifted slowly. I watched them climb up and over the top. After nearly fifty days of labor, it never really entered my mind that I could take a day off. As it turned out, I would today.

Back at the cabin I picked up the saw I had flung to one side in my wild

▲ *Dick at Spike's cabin. A lonesome aura. It needed someone to live in it.*

▲ *The head of the upper lake showing the estuary of Beaver Creek and the backdrop of towering crags.*

▸ Browned trout filets, sourdough biscuits, and honey for the first fry of the spring. ▾ A stack of sourdough pancakes drizzled with syrup and topped with bacon. ▾▸ A gathering of Dall sheep ewes browsing a high slope.

▴ Dick and transportation beached on the lower lake. Getting the kinks out from the paddling and losing himself in the panorama.

▲▲ *Felling and peeling the white spruce cabin logs.* ▲ *Bedding the side foundation logs in the beach gravel cabin site. Soon the cabin will be born.*

▲ These simple hand tools will challenge anyone's self-reliance.

▲▶ Notice how the notches fit snugly over the tops of the logs below them, as if fused.

▶ Dick thumps a gouge chisel with a spruce chunk mallet to fashion a perfect notch.

▼▶ He uses a sharp axe to even the picture window base.

▲ *The eave logs complete the side walls. With the kitchen window and picture window cut out, the structure is now ready for the gable ends to be framed.*

◄ *Much trimming to do. The framework improves with a "haircut" of the log ends.*

▲▲ *Dick readies the roof poles for installation.* ▲ *With the poles in place, the slots between the pole ends under the eaves need to be filled in. These fillers should be called "squirrel frustrators."*

▲ *A man-powered lumbermill. Ripping a board from a log is a workout for the right arm.*

▲ *A time-out with my double-edged beauty, pleased with what has been accomplished. Chips littered like fallen leaves. Enjoyed thinking about what I had done to make reality out of a dream.*

▲ Roof all tar papered and waiting for polyethylene.
I like the view from my picture window.

► My fireplace form is in place to support the arch.

▼ Chimney between purlin log and ridge pole rising
around my collapsible flue form.

▲ *My Dutch door works as slick as a door on a bank vault. Notice how the wooden hinges crafted from stumps extend like battens over the planks.*

▲ *Installing an organic roof from the forest floor source. Sections will grow together. Notice the mullions in the Mylar picture window and the driftwood sculpture behind the "panes."*

▲ *The cabin nestles among spruces below snow-frosted Crag Mountain. The beach needs attention.*

dash to get a look at the wolves, intending to get back to work. I took one last peek through the scope, though, and there no more than 100 yards from where the wolves had climbed was a cow caribou. She was standing with her head down fighting insects. This seemed very strange.

I loaded my camera gear and started up the trail to the hump. Just before reaching the top I saw a reddish object in the low brush ahead. The wolves had made a kill. There were the remains of a young cow. The three wolves had nearly devoured her. All that was left was the backbone part of the rib cage, part of one front shoulder, and most of the neck. The lower part of the head to the top of the eyes was eaten away. The lower jaw bones were stripped clean. Back straps and ribs all cleaned, too. The skin was badly torn and pulled down over the front leg as you would peel back a rubber glove. They had downed her fifty yards up the hill and scattered paunch, skin, and lungs along the trail to where she now lay.

The other caribou was nowhere to be seen. Wondering if I would see the killers again, I followed the trail high above Hope Creek, through patches of wildflowers. Many forget-me-nots, wild geraniums, dwarf fireweed, paintbrush, and wild celery. The breeze was at my back.

As I topped a ridge along a dry wash, a wolf came up from the other side, thirty or forty paces away. It was the light-colored one, staring at me head-on. She whirled and dropped over the edge. I scrambled forward to get a better look. She crossed a rocky slide and stopped on a grassy place to look back, tail down and head high. Then in a wink she was gone.

I walked the trail to the mouth of the big basin below the glacier, and sat down to glass the surrounding country. On a grassy slope was a big brown rock. Sometimes those big brown rocks move. I slipped out of my pack, lay on my stomach, and studied the spot through the lenses. It moved. I saw a bear's head raise, his muzzle tossing and testing the wind. Maybe I could get some pictures.

By the time I climbed a steep pitch, the bear was digging for squirrels. I watched him chase a squirrel in a big circle. He sprawled on his belly and worked at something held between his forepaws. All the time I was taking pictures. He lumbered down by the noisy stream, up through a willow patch, and bobbed on over the skyline.

The sun was warm and there were no insects about. I nearly fell asleep, thinking about what I had seen this day. I could have killed them all. I thought of the season that would soon open, of the men the season would bring to do just that. Kill, shake hands with the guide, and stand with hands in their pockets while he skins out the hide or saws off the skull and antlers and perhaps a quarter or two of meat, not even bothering to open the carcass. The wolves had done a better job.

While I was away, the rabbit changed his menu. He cleaned half a row of rutabagas. Bet he never tasted them before, either.

■ *July 20th*. White frost on the potato leaves. They wilted a bit with the warming of the sun.

On the way back from the hump last evening I packed some meat scraps and the antlers and skull of the wolf-killed caribou. The camp robbers were busy now on the meat scraps. There was something the wolves overlooked. I sawed through the skull to remove the antlers and there it was, the brains. I put them into a pan of salt water to soak and would have them for supper.

Put my table top, counter top, counter lower shelf, and shelf over the door together, using half-inch plugs driven into the holes on the edges of the boards. Each plug was coated with glue.

A surprise—Babe again. He brought a couple gallons of nails, spuds, onions, some fresh head lettuce, bananas, three pairs of pants, and still no polyethylene. I hadn't expected him so soon. I guess if you learn not to expect much, you won't be disappointed too often.

After Babe left, the boss hunter made two trips in. Lots of traffic today at Twin Lakes. Must be the forecast of a big season.

This evening the table and shelves are very solid. Mighty good glue.

Supper of caribou brains fried with corn meal, eggs, onions, salt, and pepper in bacon grease. And sourdough biscuits, too. That's eating high off the caribou.

■ *July 21st.* Today will be known as the day of the golden sunrise. Fast-moving fleecy clouds sailing through melted butter. A beautiful sight to watch. I was late having my hotcakes and bacon.

■ *July 22nd.* Cloudy and still.

Two months now since I started the cabin. Lots of nailing on the roof poles today. More finish work on the furniture and the cabin interior. Too windy for the roof job in the afternoon.

■ *July 23rd.* Clouds moving at a good rate of speed out of the southeast. A warm breeze.

A day to hang the door. I checked and rechecked my hinges to see that they were in line. I put the door into the opening and fastened the top and bottom hinges. Swings good but squeaks a bit. Some soap will fix that. Now to fasten number two and three hinges. Number three wasn't good enough so I pried it off and planed the seating surface. That was about right so I daubed on some glue and nailed it fast. The door works quiet and easy, with all four hinges secure. I could leave it alone or cut it in two for a Dutch door, which I had intended it to be. Let's cut her in two and see what happens.

I pulled the hinge pins, set the door on edge and sawed it nearly through. Then I put it back, inserted the hinge pins and carefully finished the cut. I swung it back. Happy day! Not perfect but plenty close for rural work. Now I had a Dutch door and a real fancy-looking door at that. With soap on the joints and pins, it is entirely silent. Works just as slick as a door on a bank vault. I must devise a latch for it, not just buttons and hooks like a barn door.

I cut my table legs to length, planed my counter top and shelves, and gave the whole works a coat of varnish. This layout is beginning to take shape.

■ *July 24th.* After supper last night I took the casting rod and the fly rod down to Hope Creek. The grayling were feeding greedily, fins and tails swirling all over the surface. A fish snapped the fly from the leader the very first cast. I didn't have another fly with me so I switched to the casting rod and the battered old Super-Duper lure dangling from the end of it. Wham—a heavy strike in the fast water and the tip hoopled. The fish darted this way and that until I finally slid him onto the stones, a handsome grayling all aglitter with silver, purple, and blue. Seventeen and a quarter inches long, enough for my needs. I watched the grayling feast on what the current brought them. What a sight it would be to put on a wet suit and mask and visit the grayling at their evening banquet down under.

Flat calm this morning and high clouds. I gave some thought to the fireplace I was going to make. I had just the log for the mantel all picked out. It was weathered a silver-gray color. I fastened it to the wall with pegs so I can saw them off when I get ready to lay up the rock. That will be an interesting project.

Supper was interrupted by a bear I spotted foraging on the upper Cowgill benches. As I often do, I had taken my binoculars off the hook for an inspection of the slopes and I caught up with the bear, not a big one. He looked like he was wearing a wig. His winter coat was loose, long and dangling from back and sides, and his new dark coat was trying to take over. He pawed over some boulders that bounced down the slope and into the spruce timber. Burned my biscuits and wilted the fireweed salad but it was worth the price.

■ *July 25th.* The camp robbers visited early. I dug out some caribou scraps, and one of the birds finally swooped in and grabbed one of them from my fingers.

I need more storage space in my cabin, something other than cans and boxes, like a closet bureau with doors on the front closing toward each other. I spent the day ripping boards out of logs. I made six hinges out of gas-can tin, then time ran out on me. I will finish it in the morning.

I am nearly moved in now.

Thought I would catch my supper at the creek mouth before heading back to Spike's cabin. A strike right off, but it got away and must have told every fish in the pool about its narrow escape because I never got another touch.

A warm evening and my sourdoughs puffed up like balloons. Light and heavenly.

▪ *July 26th.* A good morning to paddle across the lake to my straight-pole patch. When will this pole business end? I need some for my closet bureau and some to hold the moss down on the woodshed roof.

I cut more poles than I needed. Good straight poles are handy to have standing by. Back with the load before nine o'clock, and before long I finished the closet bureau started yesterday. Its shelves will hold lots of clothes. Room for some small odds and ends, too. The doors open out, close together, and stay shut tight with a twist of the wood cleat over their edges.

Now I need a window. With half-inch by half-inch mullions I divided the window frame into nine pane sections. Storm window plastic was then anchored fast with masking tape on the outside of the muttons. Handiwrap was similarly taped on the inside and the air was trapped between the layers. Presto—a poor man's thermopane.

▪ *July 27th.* How clear it is through my big window! All of a sudden the cabin has more character.

I climbed the hump and filled a can with blueberries. They are at their best with raindrops on them, but I enjoyed them sugared for dessert this evening.

Just before I broke out of the timber, I startled a mother spruce grouse with about six youngsters the size of quail. Such a hurtling in all directions! She stayed on the ground, however, pussyfooting on the carpet of moss and making low clucking sounds without opening her bill at all. Her throat feathers swelled as the low sounds came out.

I spotted a little one balancing on a bough. As I approached, it squatted nervously, stretched its neck down below the level of its body, wobbled its head, teetered, crouched lower, and stretched higher as if to say, "Hey, Ma, what do I do now?" I backed away to avoid further confusion of the family.

▪ *July 28th.* My camp robber friend appeared at breakfast and stole a snip of bacon right out of my plate as I sat in the doorway.

I must say I really like my window.

I took a charcoal stick and sketched the fireplace chimney on the logs, then cut a big piece of cardboard to the pitch of the roof and set it up on top. I was pleased with how a chimney would look, and the moss on the roof will improve the whole effect even more. Inside I tacked more cardboard under the log mantel and drew a fireplace on it.

I nailed the molding in tight around my window and plugged the cracks in the door with oakum. Then I chinked the toilet end of the woodshed and packed in some gravel from the beach to cover the floor.

Tomorrow I will make a latch for my Dutch door.

■ *July 29th.* The wind rattled through the trees last night, and the lake was noisy. Clouds coming from the southeast this morning, a mile a minute.

Ready to construct my super door latch. I would use a wooden disc with a lug on one side to engage in the door casing, and a shaft squared to take the handles.

Now I needed a lock. Any old housedog of a bear could push the handle down and open the door. I augered a hole through the door, a third of its diameter, cutting a notch in the wooden disc. When the door handle was turned it engaged the disc and the door was locked. I would like to see a bear try to figure it out, but I suppose he would just solve the problem by wiping the door clean from the wooden hinges.

A wild lake all day. Whitecaps chasing each other.

■ *July 30th.* Last evening I went blueberrying on the Cowgill benches. I found a good patch, and when the can was nearly full, I noticed a movement across the creek. Something yellow and brown—a big bear and not 200 yards away. While watching him, I instinctively turned around to see if maybe something was watching me.

He was picking berries and really giving a demonstration, his big head swinging this way and that and bobbing up and down at the same time. Leaves and berries were being stripped off with that long tongue. I finished filling my can, then eased over to the edge of the creek bank and sat down for a closer look. A breeze coming from him to me and the noise of the creek made the seat perfect. I watched him eat his way into a grove of cottonwoods on the steep side of the canyon. It was after ten o'clock when I dropped down off the bench and walked through the spruce timber with bears on my mind.

A tin bending day. Made a water bucket, a wash pan, a dishpan, a flour pan, and storage cans. My cabin kitchen is shaping up.

■ *July 31st.* The last day of July and I don't believe I saw new snow during the entire month.

Today would be the day to set up the stove and do some more tin bending. I dug the stove out of a corner of Spike's cabin. When I saw the old relic in good light, I almost chickened out of the project. It was the sorriest looking stove I ever saw. A half-inch gap along the sides under the top, one door hinge unstuck. I packed it down through the brush and put it on my stove stand. Then I put up my new stovepipe and made ready to touch it off.

First I packed a bucket of small rocks to put under the grate, then gravel to fill the grate. It would take a long time to get ashes enough to hold a fire. I stuffed in some shavings and some chips and struck a match. The flames grew out along the sides under the top and I thought, "This will never do". And then the smoke found the smoke stack and my troubles were over. In spite of its looks it did a fine job heating water. I was pleasantly surprised. Now to make it look professional I would need a Chinese hat for the top of the chimney pipe, so I got busy with tools and tin and had one on in short order.

Found a way to get paper and stickum off a gas can. Boil it in hot soapy water. The label is on to stay, but it can't stand that treatment.

I needed a big wooden spoon to dip hotcake batter onto the griddle. One spoonful, one hotcake. In the woodpile I found scraps of stump wood that looked suitable. It took no more than an hour to turn out a good-looking spoon. I must make a wooden bowl or two later on.

Cool breeze and the insects are no problem today.

Tomorrow is the big day. I will load all my remaining gear into the canoe and paddle down to my new home. A calm sea will help for this voyage.

▪ *August 1st.* The lake dead calm. A perfect moving day. A camp robber, visiting me for breakfast, came inside. I wonder what his range is? Will he find me at the new cabin?

I worked clockwise around Spike's cabin, set out everything that I wanted to go, and packed it down to the beach. Then I cleaned up the cabin that had been home, scrubbed the counter, the shelf, and the woodwork of the stove stand. I glanced at Spike's sign and was satisfied I had complied. Everything in order and better than I found it.

I loaded the canoe and paddled down to my new quarters. Everything found its place and there was lots of room for everything, not a cluttered look at all. Some items to make, such as a knife holder to fasten on the wall.

Suddenly it happened, the worst accident of my cabin building career. The piece of wood I was working turned, and I raked my thumb with the newly sharpened ripsaw. Blood ran all over the place. I hurried down and stuck my thumb into the cold lake, watched the water turn from green to red, then doped up the gash, wrapped a rag around it, anchored it with a piece of tape, and went back to work.

Burned my sourdoughs a bit on the bottom, but they were good anyway. It will take a few trial runs to get used to my antique range.

First night on my new bunk. Five inches of foam rubber will make it just about right. I can hear Hope Creek real plain. That will be a pleasant sound to go to sleep by.

The lake water is good, but now I pack it from Hope Creek and I think there is none better that I have ever tasted. I like to think of the high places it comes from.

I lit the Coleman lantern this evening. A bright, friendly glow in the wilderness, the warmth of home.

▪ *August 2nd.* Best sleep in a long time. The sound of the waves lapping the gravel beach and the never-ending rustle of Hope Creek until freeze-up. No better sleeping pill.

The stove did a fine job on the hotcakes this morning and my wooden spoon is just right. Perfect-sized cakes every time.

I must have a stool outside to set things on when opening the door. A ten-inch slice from a twelve-inch-diameter log, and legs augered into one side. Gave the legs a flare so the stool won't tip when I step on it. Why not a couple more thin slices from the log, and plane them smooth? Now I had place mats and hot pads to save my plastic tablecloth.

That Babe! He landed and had things unloaded at Spike's cabin before I could get to him. We put the gear back into the plane and taxied down to my beach.

He'd brought the polyethylene at last, more than enough, and plenty of grub. Also a package from my sister, Florence.

I watched Babe's eyes move with approval over the cabin walls. "A nice place," he said. "A real nice place."

"Like heaven," I said.

He just looked at me and slowly wagged his head.

I waved to him as he took off down country into the rainy fog, heading home.

Good news. Spike and Hope want me to take the stove from their cabin. They will bring in another one sometime. In nothing flat I paddled down to get it. I took out some of the ashes before hauling it down, then out went that sorry-looking other monster, rocks, gravel, and all. Some spikes into the top of my stove stand and the old reliable was soon in place. I scratched a match. She took off like a gut-shot cat. A welcome sound, as welcome as having one's wife return to full duty after an operation (I imagine).

The biscuits puffed up just right and baked to a turn. All is going well. Tomorrow I can work full time on the roof.

■ *August 3rd.* Not the breath of a breeze. Just the kind of day I need to put the polyethylene on the roof. Even the trace of a breeze makes it want to float.

A few minor details in preparing the felt paper, then I unrolled the polyethylene and tucked the edges to get at least four thicknesses to tack through, and I fastened her down.

Next I built a carrying rack for the moss. Made it out of poles in a frame two feet by three feet. I filed the blade of my round-point shovel and I was ready for the moss-cutting detail. I had a good moss bed all picked out. I cut out rectangles about eighteen inches by thirty-six inches, and eight inches thick. Two chunks double-decked on the rack made a good load. Once around the edge of the roof, and the cabin took on a new look. Before it seemed as though the windows were too close under the eaves, but the thick roof fixes that now.

By late afternoon I finished the lake side of the roof. I got to thinking of blueberries for dessert. Thirty-five minutes later my picking can was full.

A beautiful, still evening. The cabin is beginning to look as though it belongs.

■ *August 4th.* A surprise last evening just as it was getting a bit on the dark side—Babe in the old Stinson. As soon as the prop stopped, out he bounced from his little door up forward.

"Man, am I ever tired," he said. "Been flying for ten hours. Moved the prospectors' camp to Farewell. Moved everything. Coming back it got so dark I couldn't see the gas gauge, and the last time I saw it, the needle was on the wrong side of the glass."

He had some gas cached here. He would stay the night and gas up in the morning.

I had the fire going the next morning when Babe said, "Sure don't take long to stay all night here."

Suspenders hanging, Babe washed up. I could hear him sputtering water through his moustache. After hotcakes and bacon we hauled the gas that was cached in the brush and poured the fuel into the tank of the Stinson, which looked like a Greyhound bus compared to the T-Craft. Big doors, big windows, and room inside for five fifty-gallon barrels.

The old girl was balky at first. She had made many starts yesterday. The 120 oil made her stiff. A primer line had broken and, even after some repair work, still didn't prime too well. Finally she stuttered and shuddered into life. I watched her taxi out into the lake. She lifted easily. I wondered what they were thinking back in Port Alsworth when Babe didn't return last night.

Back to the roof job. It seems I have cleared two acres of moss and still the roof isn't covered.

Hard to believe, but I have all the moss in place at last. The cabin suddenly has even more character. This roof has helped more than any one thing to give the cabin a finished look. Now for the poles to hold down the moss. Four poles on a side will look better than three, I figure.

Babe brought in some fresh groceries that needed refrigeration. I had dug down a foot into the moss yesterday and found frost. Why not dig a hole and put in a gas-can box, then use my moss-carrying rack loaded with moss for a cover? I think that will do the job. I must put the thermometer in there to find out the temperature.

Clouding up down country. May bring rain tomorrow. I'll never hear it with all the moss on the roof to deaden the drops when they hit.

■ *August 5th.* No rain.

I finished mossing the woodshed roof. Then I cut and notched the poles to lay over the moss and fastened them down. The woodshed is now complete and looks it.

I need more poles for the cabin roof and also to make a long ladder for a meat tree. Only one place to find poles like that: the upper end of the lake, a four-mile paddle each way.

Found the poles easy enough. Took me an hour and a half to paddle home against a light breeze. It was after nine before I got my supper dishes done. A real productive day.

■ *August 6th.* Clear and calm. Almost too warm. I would like to see some rain. The waterfall across the lake is about to run dry.

Today would be a small detail day. Window-closing handles and latches. Hinges to make and put up a ten-inch by twelve-inch shelf on the wall for my water bucket. Many wooden pegs to replace nails to hang things on. The poles to peel that I hauled yesterday.

Thinking ahead for the winter season, I found three trees spaced about right and put two green spruce poles in traction among them to get the proper curved shape for sled runners in case I decided to build a sled.

In and out of the cabin all day. A kettle of red beans on the fire. Put in bacon rind and bacon chunks and onions and all my favorite seasonings. That's the kind of cooking to do in the wilderness, something that cooks while you do something else and don't have to stand over.

The thermometer in my cooler box under the moss reads forty degrees. Under the really deep moss I am sure the temperature would read even lower. And here it is close to eighty degrees today.

■ *August 7th.* The sun is getting up later.

Lots of mountains to climb over before it strikes the cabin.

Today I put the poles on the cabin roof to hold the moss in place until it grows together. I converted the three-legged stool to a four-legger. A near fall convinced me this had to be done. Then I built a three-shelf open rack for outside the door to set butter, blueberries, and such away from the heat of the cabin.

Really warm today, too warm. I ran a check on temperatures. Forty degrees in my cooler box, seventy-eight degrees in the cabin, ninety-four degrees in the sun, and the lake water sixty-six degrees in the shallows. That last reading really surprised me, and I promptly went for a swim. The surface water was almost comfortable, but I could feel the iciness that lurked just below.

I glued corrugated cardboard to my wooden place mats. They look rustic and are good insulation for hot pots.

Small planes beginning to appear, flying the peaks and those high pastures looking for game. The season will open on the tenth. I wonder what that meat costs a pound?

This is the warmest day I have ever seen here at the lakes. I didn't even build a fire.

■ *August 8th.* Really had a time here this afternoon. I looked up from my letter-writing to chew on my pen end and peer down the lake through the big window. For a moment I thought I was having hallucinations. Lots of motion and here comes a brown bear up my path.

He was nosing the gravel as he shuffled toward me, getting bigger all the time. He looked somewhat small for a brown, but he would have been big for a black. Abruptly he stopped and flipped his muzzle at the wind currents. I waited for him to wince as the man-scent struck him, and bolt with a crashing into the brush.

No such reaction at all. He just ambled unconcerned past my big window in the direction of the rear of the cabin. No more had he gone out of sight when I heard sounds that brought me right up out of the chair. That character was trying to climb up the corner of the cabin and onto my new roof!

This would never do. I slid the .357 magnum from its holster on the wall and stepped out the door. No bear could I see on the roof, so I yelled and touched off a round that exploded like a thunderclap.

It didn't have the expected result. Around the corner came the bear in four-paw drive. I scrambled for the door, pulled it shut and gripped a fist down hard on the handle. The bear came slamming against the planks. I felt his weight bulging the upper door and heard the rake of his claws.

What kind of a bear was this? The noises he was making didn't sound friendly at all. In fact, they sounded downright psychopathic. His guttural complaints trailed off and I knew he was moving away. Through the small window I watched him poke toward the woodshed. He explored the area thoroughly, standing on his hind legs, teetering and snuffling along the front eave. He was one curious bruin.

Was he going to try climbing up the woodshed? Maybe it would take the heavy artillery to scare him off. I loaded the ought-six, opened the window, and rested the barrel on the sill. Then I turned loose a rebel yell.

He must have been a reincarnation of Jeb Stuart. He spun with unbelievable quickness and came on like the cavalry. I drove a slug into the path in front of him, making the gravel fly. He put on the brakes, whirled in retreat, then stopped, rising to his full height as if trying to peer beyond the cabin logs and solve the strangeness there. Noiselessly he dropped to all fours with an almost fluid movement and was gone.

Less than five minutes later, here he came from another direction, this time toward the front of the cabin, stalking—silently and ominously.

I didn't like it at all. There was an orneriness about him I could feel. I couldn't have pets like this running around the place. The best thing to do would be to shoot him, skin him out, and write a letter to Fish and Game.

He must have picked up warning vibrations. Off he went in a sudden huff, slinging his forepaws in pigeon-toed strides until the willows closed behind him. I checked the latch on my door and went back to my letter writing.

This evening I went on bear patrol. No sign of him. Just passing through, I hope. I think he has headed out of the country. I guess I made myself a pretty good door at that. One thing I can't understand though: If that character wanted in, how come he passed up the big window?

Let's have some rain. Every day I have been watering what is left of my garden.

I need an outside bench. Some slabs from my board ripping operations are available. Well, what do you know about that? I got carried away. That bench just grew and grew into a small table and a rather handsome one at that.

The top is fifteen inches by thirty-two inches. It stands twenty-eight inches off the ground.

Now for a general cleanup of the area. I moved all my scrap to the woodshed or under the trees nearby. Some I would be able to use so I kept them separate. I found one four-inch-diameter log end that wasn't split, so I augered a one-and-a-half-inch hole into one end, three inches deep, and planed it smooth. Then I cut the piece down to a three-and-three-quarter-inch length. A dandy holder for pens and pencils.

I cut the brush under my clothesline and raked up two buckets of wood chips. Now the cabin looks landscaped.

A good day, like all days, at Twin Lakes.

■ *August 9th.* No sign of that psycho in the fur coat. He's far away, I hope.

Heavy gray clouds. Might bring some rain. The lake is rising slightly. Must be the warm weather has been acting on the snowfields in the high mountains. No sign of game at all. Strange I don't see a caribou on the slopes now and then.

While cultivating the garden, I rolled out a potato the size of a walnut. The green onions look respectable. The crops to grow at Twin Lakes are rhubarb, potatoes, lettuce, green onions, and radishes.

I have decided that no more chips and sawdust will be made in front of the cabin. I scraped up the entire area slick and clean and dressed it properly with a new coat of beach gravel.

Fishing at the mouth of Hope Creek has been poor. Where have the fish gone?

The wind is strong this evening, and the lake is churning as if it wants to turn itself loose.

■ *August 10th.* Gray clouds racing across the sky. This must be a real blow on the Gulf of Alaska.

Today, among other things, I'd build a butcher's block for outside the door. A ten-inch length of eleven-inch-diameter log with three legs. I finished it in short order. Then from the same log I sliced off two five-eighths-inch slabs cut on a diagonal and planed them to bring out the grain and the growth rings. They will make proper decorations for the wall or the fireplace mantel. I coated them with clear shellac. I shellacked my plaster wolf track, too.

The rest of the morning I spent supplying wood for the stove. I sawed up pole ends and short sections of logs left over from the building program.

After lunch I bucked up a tree that had blown across the trail last winter. I packed in the log sections and chopped up the limbs into stove lengths. Sharp tools make wood cutting a pleasure.

I am getting hungry for a fish. Decided in late afternoon I would have to catch one. After many casts beyond the gravel bar at the mouth of Hope Creek, I was onto a fish. I worked him easy, for I was fish hungry and didn't want to lose the grayling. A rock on the head stopped his flopping. His colors faded quicker than a sunset. I could see him browning in the pan as I dressed him out and left his entrails for the birds.

Picked some blueberries but found very few cranberries.

■ *August 11th.* A big caribou bull on the Cowgill Bench. Very dark, with his cape starting to whiten and the velvet graying on his antlers. The insects were giving him fits.

The camp robbers have still not come to the cabin.

Stayed close to home today. The boss hunter has brought hunters. Two-legged animals will be prowling the hills for a spell.

■ *August 12th.* The spruce boughs are glistening with raindrops. The land had a bath last night.

Calm after the big blow of yesterday. I decided to take a trip down to the lower end of the lake. I could use a fish or two.

An easy paddle down. An arctic tern sliced above, hovering to look me over, his breast picking up a pale blue cast from the water. Rags of fog are strewn about the high peaks. I pulled the canoe up high on the gravel of the lower end. Fish were breaking. One that looked two feet long rolled on the surface. If I could only sink a hook into that one—but no luck after many casts. To make matters worse, the breeze was coming up strong, and down the lake at that. One last try. I let the lure sink way down and twitched it toward me. Wham! A heavy fish but not much fight. More color than I have ever seen in a lake trout. Bright yellow fins and belly, big lemon spots against gray-green sides. This one should break my record of nineteen inches. I had my fish but now I was in trouble. Whitecaps all over the place and that seventh wave a big one. I could leave the canoe tied to the brush and high on the beach and then walk the three miles back, or give it a try.

I shoved the canoe out into the wind, crouched low with knees spread against the bottom. It was a battle. I finally made it to a bight in the shoreline near Low Pass Creek, and it was a relief to get behind the steep beach out of the wind. I slid the canoe into the shallows, tied her fast, and gorged myself in a blueberry patch.

Still blowing. I tied one end of my long line to the bow and the other end about two-thirds of the way back toward the stern. Holding the line in the middle, I kept adjusting until the bow of the canoe was farther from shore than the stern, and started walking the beach. It worked real well for a time, until it got broadside to the wind and was blown ashore. Then I got in to paddle to the next favorable section of towing beach.

I was getting home, but it was a slow process. I got slowed down even more when I hit a section of no beach and big boulders. I took to the open water and battled my way. As I passed the boss hunter's cabin, I saw something hanging on the meat pole, with birds flying around it. The fresh meat looked like a front quarter. No other sign of life around the cabin.

By the time I made my beach, I had had a workout. My trout measured nineteen inches on the nose. It was a female loaded with eggs. I fried them in bacon grease with lots of corn meal, a dose of Tabasco sauce, some poultry seasoning, salt, and pepper. When the eggs got hot, they commenced to pop like popcorn and flew every which way when I lifted the lid covering the pan. They were different.

■ *August 13th.* It could rain today without too much trouble.

I made a paper-towel rack out of some spruce stock. Two end pieces supported a dowel that could be easily removed. Next I made a curtain rod out of a skinny piece of driftwood and hung the burlap curtains sister Florence had sent.

Clean up my beach—that was a job that needed doing. I wanted to make it a beach that a pilot would enjoy coming into. I piled the driftwood in one pile, the rocks and boulders in another, and waded out to pick the large stones from the bottom to pile them also. When I finished, I was sure I had the best plane-landing place in both lakes.

A heavy fish splashed just out from the cabin. Have the sockeyes arrived? I must watch for them.

A little later I looked up from applying a coat of Varathane on my furniture to see a scarlet fish with a green head slice through a wave. It is the end of a long journey for them. They will spawn and die. Their escape from the can is a very brief reprieve.

This evening I sat on my driftwood pile admiring my cabin. Pale blue wood smoke rose up through the dark boughs of the spruce, and beyond, looming huge and majestic, the jagged peak of Crag Mountain. The cabin was complete now except for the fireplace and, maybe later on, a cache up on poles. It was a good feeling just sitting and reflecting, a proud inner feeling of something I had created with my own hands. I don't think I have ever accomplished anything as satisfying in my entire life.

– Camp Meat –

■ *August 27th.* A frosty morning.

I picked up two rams in the spotting scope. They were feeding on a grassy bench high above Glacier Creek, at the base of a rock slide. Suddenly five more rams appeared, big curved horns against the blue sky. It wasn't long before I heard an outboard motor, and there droning toward Glacier Creek in a small boat were two hunters. Other eyes had been watching those rams, too.

This would bear watching. I could use some sheep meat, and if those boys made a kill up that high, they would surely leave most of the meat on the mountain. I watched them beach, shoulder their packboards, sling their rifles, and head up the stony creek bed. They were off on a search-and-destroy mission.

From time to time I checked the hunters through the big lens. They were making very slow progress. The big rams were dropping down lower, a string of white dots on the thread of a trail. I almost wished I could warn them.

I decided to pick a can of blueberries while waiting for the main event, so I packed the spotting scope and tripod up to the hump behind the cabin. Picking had been slow, and just as I discovered a patch loaded with large berries, I heard shots rolling down from the high places. Six shots, one echoing on the heels of the other. They must have been shooting at extreme range hoping for a hit. I saw five sheep trailing across the mountain. There had been seven.

I picked up the hunters on the rock slide. I saw one ram tumbling down the steep incline. The men started another on its way, over and over, legs flailing the air. When the rams stopped, the hunters worked down to where the white blobs lay and started them rolling again.

What a way to treat a set of horns and cape, not to mention the meat. Finally the bodies came to rest on a stretch of level ground. The boys decided this would be the butchering place and went at it. I concentrated on the berry patch. I knew where to find some sheep meat in the morning.

Back at the cabin in late afternoon I glanced into the spotting scope at intervals to see how the hunters were doing. They were coming down with heavy loads, stopping to rest often. They will remember that trip up and down the mountain for a long time.

About seven o'clock the outboard started up, and two very tired men were only the width of the lake away from calling it a day.

■ *August 28th.* Clear and frosty at 4:30 A.M. At 5:45 I embarked on Operation Sheep Meat. Flour sacks, meat saw, and packboard were loaded into the canoe. On the trip across, the sun didn't strike me until I turned the canoe bottom up on the gravel beach.

At 6:40 I took off up the creek. I followed game trails and beat the brush toward the steep cottonwood-covered slope. The cottonwoods were nearly all of one size and as straight as telephone poles. High ferns, highbush cranberries, and fireweed, but none of it blooming now. The blue sky showed through the branches. A part of living has got to be climbing through a grove of cottonwoods when the leaves are shivering in gold.

The wind blew cold from the glacier, and patches of fog poured down as I neared the end of the climb.

I found the two rams lying about twenty yards apart. More meat had been taken than I figured, but neither of the carcasses had been opened. I dressed them both out and couldn't find anything wrong with the meat. The cold mountain air had kept it chilled.

I made up a load of two front quarters, the tenderloins, the ribs, neck, and some pieces of sheepskin. I sawed off two of the feet, just to have, and tucked them into the load. Then I sat down with my back to it, worked my arms into the straps, and shrugged the heavy pack to my shoulders. I rose to my feet and, with my walking stick, picked my way toward home.

Whitecaps were on the lake when I reached the canoe. Why is it that the wind always blows up the lake when I must cross it going down? They were big swells, too. I remember my commercial fishing days. Before a blow, the big swells came.

I was halfway across the lake before the breeze picked up, and by the time I reached my beach the wind was blasting. Had I been another fifteen minutes later I would have been hunting for a hole.

I sorted the meat and hung it high from the branch of a tree. I fleshed out the two pieces of hide and soaked the blood from the white hair. Then I prepared the ribs for supper. They were flavorful, but I was sure of one thing: The big ram they came from had roamed the mountains for a long time.

■ *August 29th.* Today I would smoke the sheep meat.

The other day I had passed the boss hunter's camp. I saw six quarters of meat hanging uncovered from the meat pole. At forty feet the stench came to me. The wolves had done a better job. My meat would be properly cared for.

I set up a big tripod of poles over the smoke tunnel outlet, hung the entire batch of meat in the teepee, covered the structure with the heavy plastic, and touched off a fire at the other end. I heaped the fire with dead cottonwood and peeled alder. Soon the smoke was pouring from the tunnel outlet, and the meat inside the plastic tent was lost in the vapor.

Dug three hills of spuds today. Not record breakers for size but they had real smooth skins.

I must add an accessory to the john. That rascal of a spruce squirrel just went berserk with a small roll of toilet paper. He packed it off with him and bannered it up and down and over the boughs. What a mess! We will have no more of that. The toilet paper is now stuck on the spruce peg as usual, but it is capped with a coffee can. Let's see if the little scamp can figure that one out.

While transferring my meat from the smoker back to the meat tree, I noticed an occasional sockeye salmon break water. A pretty sight, those bright red fish arcing in the sun against the green water. Lots of mileage on them since they entered the fresh water. They struggled against the currents of the Mulchatna and the Chilikadrotna and finally into the Twins.

I covered the meat with a poncho and stored the ladder. Now the meat should be able to take it if there is a rise in temperature.

■ *September 6th.* For some time now I had my plans for the fireplace drawn up, and they looked satisfactory. Yesterday Babe came in with the big Stinson and brought, among other things, six sacks of cement, a garden hoe, and an empty fifty-gallon drum, but no lime. Without it the mortar might not stick well to the stone. That bothered me but I will go ahead with construction anyway. I hope there will be enough cement.

A familiar sound rained down from the sky this morning as I was picking blueberries up on the benches. I looked up and there they were, beating their way up country against the wind—about forty big gray, black-necked honkers.

This would be the morning to start the fireplace. I had been packing flat stones from the bed of Hope Creek for the past few days. These would be for the base. The sight of those geese made me even more anxious to get the project under way.

First thing, I would need a tub in which to mix mortar. That's where the fifty-gallon drum made its contribution. With a wide Sears chisel, I cut the drum in two. Such a racket! The edges of the tub were rolled and hammered flat. The garden hoe completed the kit. Next a good gas-can carrier to pack the rocks and mortar in. I cut a gas can lengthwise a generous six inches deep, then fashioned a cradle of light poles with rugged handles. I set the gas-can tub into this and nailed it fast. Result—a sturdy rig.

After checking my plan several times, I marked the logs for cutting. I almost hated the thought of cutting into those cabin logs that I had fitted with such care, but it had to be done.

I transferred my rock pile from the beach up to the back of the cabin, the colorful rocks laid out side by side so I could see them individually, the rest in two piles, one on each side of the fireplace location.

I dug out for the base, allowing for lots of rock in a solid footing to eliminate danger of it tipping in time or settling.

Tomorrow I will see the hole cut and some stone put into place. I'm not sure how it will go without the lime.

■ *September 7th.* Temperature forty-three degrees at 4:30 A.M.

The lake was moon still. A good morning to haul some sand. Up at the point was a good supply, two grades, fine and coarse. I loaded two gas-can boxes, my new carrier, and two gas-can buckets into the canoe and paddled through the thin fog. I could see tracks of caribou at the water's edge.

Four loads of sand. That was enough for a start. I won't cut that hole in the back of the cabin too high until I find out how this rock laying is going to go. I took out sections from the two bottom logs. That gave me plenty of room to lay the base. Took out some rock and dirt on the outside and I was ready for mortar. Three shovels of fine sand, two of coarse, and one heaping shovelful of cement, just about the right amount for a good mix. I dumped all the rock I could get into the six-inch-deep, four-foot by five-foot area. I used flat rocks on that part of the base extending inside the cabin. When the base was finished, I had used less than a sack of cement.

The yellow colors on the slopes of Falls Mountain are really budding up now. Those are mostly cottonwoods. They seem to prefer the sun-warmed slopes.

■ *September 8th.* A white frost and a light crust on the sand of the beach. A trace of new snow on the peaks.

I hauled three loads of sand while the lake was still. I am not overly happy with my cement. I have to screen it and then break up the hard lumps. I hesitated to take out more logs. Let's see how the outside rocks stack up first.

I spent the day on the outside. Finished the sack of cement I opened yesterday and not quite half of the second one today. The chimney is a good twelve inches high and nine inches thick. I cleaned up the joints around the rocks. So far so good. Will it stand the test of time?

There was lots of flying activity at the boss hunter's cabin and at the rough landing strip at the head of the lake.

The yellow colors across the lake are even brighter this afternoon, and with a dead-calm lake the reflections are a delight to see.

Ram stew sopped up with sourdough biscuits is mighty good eating.

■ *September 9th.* The fine weather continues. I appreciate it.

I took the plunge today. I cut the other five logs out of the back of the cabin and let the sun shine in. I sawed the opening the full forty-eight inches wide and then made two splines, one for each side of the opening, and drove a twenty-penny nail through the spline and into each log end. The splines will be imbedded in the mortar. Nine-inch jambs—an opening thirty inches across, twenty-six inches high, and twenty-four inches deep.

A picture-perfect day to work. Big, puffy white clouds in a blue sky. The slopes golden in the sun.

This evening my fireplace stands fourteen inches above the base all the way around. About another ten or twelve inches in front, and I will be ready for the arch of the opening.

Much shooting over at the boss hunter's cabin. Almost as if someone had missed a good shot because his sights were haywire, and he was making sure it wouldn't happen a second time.

In the late afternoon I paddled out on the still lake to see the reflection of my cabin. When the sun is low, it is as if the cabin is being spotted with a very bright floodlight. I am anxious to get that fireplace chimney above the roof. Then I will build a smoky fire and take a picture of the action from out here.

■ *September 10th.* Such weather I have never seen. Frosty and clear, with everything in extra-sharp focus. I should make good time today. No sand to haul, no logs to cut, no meat to cook, plenty of ram stew left and getting better all the time.

The fireplace now stands twenty-four inches behind and twenty-two in front. I must build the arch over the opening, and then on up to fill the opening. Nineteen inches to go and the hole in the back of the cabin will be plugged. At present I have a snug-fitting arrangement of corrugated cardboard that I wedge into the opening to shut out the cold air at night. I've used two sacks of cement and a third is gone from sack number three. If five sacks get me started up the chimney, I will be happy.

■ *September 11th.* Temperature twenty-nine degrees and warming. Lake water at forty-four degrees.

Today is the day to build the arch. I had given a lot of thought as to how it can be done wilderness-style. I took one of the bigger log sections I had cut from the opening and bucked off a thirty-inch length, the width of the fireplace opening. I marked one side grid-fashion, lines one-half inch between length-wise, and lines two inches apart up and down. Then I drove two nails, one in the center of the top line, the other eight inches away and toward the end on the second line.

Next I hooked the one-man cross cut sawblade at the handle under the outboard nail, and over the center nail I pulled the end of the saw down until it touched the bottom line. I traced a pencil line along the curve formed by the sawblade against the log. I moved the outboard nail to the other side of the center nail and repeated the procedure.

The result was a three-inch arch in a thirty-inch length. I roughed the log to the line with my ax and then finished it off with the jack plane. Next I flattened the ends on the underside to sit on posts I had cut from logs. I set the arch in place and spiked it to the posts. Then I braced and wedged them tight, and covered the arch with a piece of plastic.

Stones to outline the arch were on hand. The center one, pale orange and about four inches square, I had found on Emerson Creek. The rest were roughly rectangular. I mixed rich mortar, and by eleven o'clock I had my face stones in place and some filled in behind. I was quite happy with the way it turned out, so I decided to let it set the rest of the day and work on the back side.

I am starting to close in on all four sides to the throat and smoke shelf. Once past that point the chimney should climb at a rapid rate. I still have three and a third sacks of cement, which should be plenty.

I watched a Supercub land in some rough water, then take off a few minutes later in a shower of spray. A pretty fair pilot I would say. I'm happy he can't land up where the big rams are.

After supper I gathered more rocks of special shapes and sizes until it was too dark to see.

■ *September 12th.* An overcast cutting off the tops of the mountains. The frost gives them a ghostly look.

I had no idea there are so many rocks in a small fireplace. About seventy-five percent of them don't seem to fit until just the right situation turns up. One in particular I tried a dozen times before, and today it fell into place as if it was made for the spot.

Another row of stones above the arch is completed and filled in behind. That makes it a good six inches thick. I am taking it slow on the front side to let it set up properly. I'm using a stronger mixture there, too. All my stones in the front of the fireplace have been collected in my travels up and down both lakes, the high country and the low, so they are representative of the entire area.

I'm just about ready now to start forming the smoke shelf, and nearly have the sides pulled in to the point where the chimney will go straight up. It shouldn't take long after that. Three sacks of cement are gone. One more should get me to the chimney.

Building this fireplace has been just as interesting as building the cabin, and it will take me about as long as the heavy log work on the cabin, ten days.

It was real cool working bare-handed. I didn't think I could do the points as well with my old rubber work gloves on. My fingertips are worn thin and tender. I gave the old gloves a try again later on, and this evening my hands feel better because I did.

I will need more fine sand from the point tomorrow. I hope the lake flattens for the trip. Today I found the last half of the sack of cement not caked, which worked much better.

Several planes came in and left today. I think the hunters are pulling out. Soon just the Man Upstairs and I will be running this big country again, and the game will move back in.

■ *September 13th.* Thirty-two degrees at dawn. The mountains down country are white. Breezing up.

A box of very coarse beach gravel that was wet last night was frozen. When I went to mix my second batch of mortar, I noticed a few stray gobs of concrete in the tub were frozen.

I finished another course of rocks over the arch. Then I pulled the hearth in gradually to chimney size.

I tried something new that works very well. I packed in some coarse beach gravel, and when filling in between the inner and outer wall, I troweled in some mortar, dumped in as much gravel as it would stand, and puddled it in with a stick to settle it. I am now down to the required eighteen inches for width and starting the smoke shelf.

The front side is coming up to pass the smoke shelf. Now five inches between the two sides.

One more course of stones inside will plug the opening. I had thought of a stone mantel, but as yet I haven't seen any suitable stone. I may insert some three-and-one-half-inch pegs through the top course of stones and then rip a heavy slab from a good log. Then I'll plane the top of it and Varathane it as well as the face of the entire fireplace.

Tomorrow, weather permitting, I will be starting up with the chimney. Rough seas today. No chance to get sand.

■ *September 14th.* Twenty-eight degrees. Clear and frosty.

The beach gravel next to the water was frozen hard as a rock. My stones were covered with frost. The lake was calm so I hauled a load of fine sand from the point. When the sun came out from behind Crag Mountain, it warmed up the fireplace location.

Clouds are moving in like troops rushing to the front. I was just starting the straight sides of the chimney when it started to snow, flakes as big as goose feathers, but it quickly turned to rain.

I still had the face of the fireplace to finish, so I worked inside the cabin. I spaced my mantel pegs and mortared them in. Then I put in a row of small stuff to level it off. All the face needed now was to have the concrete stain removed. I wish I knew what the stone masons use. An acid of some sort, I believe. I had a little mud left, so I worked outside in the rain to use it up.

I tidied up the inside and scratched away the loose mortar from the seams with a bent nail. Then I took the braces and wedges away from the supports under the arch. I was tempted to remove the wooden arch completely because the first two seams above it were very hard. Finally I decided I had better leave it there until I completed the chimney.

I'd had a kettle of white beans on the stove all day, seasoned with everything in the cabin. I tossed in onions, potatoes, carrots, bacon and even chunks of the mountain ram, then a tablespoon of flour mixed with cold water. A regular old Midwestern bean soup to keep the sourdough biscuits company.

Fall colors are fading fast. Blueberry leaves fall away at the touch now. I must have one more good picking session.

■ *September 15th.* A faint trace of blue sky. My camp robber friend joined me for breakfast.

Today I finished the chimney throat and pulled in the sides to go up straight between the ridge log and the purlin log. While I worked over the opening, I could feel the warm air rising. That's a good sign.

Fifty inches of chimney to build now, and it should be complete. One problem—I have no flue pipe. I must build a collapsible form to act like one. If I hinge it with gas-can tin on the four sides, I can keep removing and raising it. Spacers will hold it in the rectangular position again. It will be a faster operation, and a form on the inside will make the smooth surface necessary for proper smoke flow.

My rock supply is holding up better than I expected. It looks as though I will have rocks to sell after I am finished.

■ *September 16th.* Twenty-eight degrees and the stars out.

While waiting for it to warm up, I would build my collapsible form. It required six panels of gas-can box and eighteen hinges for all four corners and the center of sides and ends. I knock the spacers out that hold it expanded, and it will contract enough so that it can be lifted and raised for the next section. Too bad there will be only two lifts to complete the chimney. Ten-thirty before I got the fool contraption completed.

It was warm working in the sun, which finally had the whole sky to itself. The mountains were a blazing white against the blue.

I still had considerable form material and braces inside the smoke shelf and throat. I may have to burn them out. My collapsible form sitting on top of all this just clears the roof on the under side.

I have changed the mortar mix to five-to-one and am getting better mortar than at four-to-one. Sifting the cement through screen wire helps considerably.

While I was working today, the camp robber swooped out of the trees and perched on my shoulder. I turned my head slowly. He was within inches of my face. "I think we'll get along fine," I said. I gave him a chunk of meat scrap, and he was gone for the day.

Well, I just couldn't put it off any longer. I got the Swede saw and sawed the posts from under the arch support but it still stuck there. I tapped it with the hammer until it broke loose. I had covered the wooden support with a piece of plastic, and the arch was smooth as glass on the underside.

Last fall from offshore in the canoe, I visualized a cabin on this spot. I could see in detail just how it would look. The fireplace has turned out the same, just as I pictured it. If I can only get rid of that cement stain! Last evening I tried a little vinegar, and it did more good than all my scrubbing with water.

■ *September 17th.* A frosty morning at twenty-three degrees. Thirty-five degrees in my cooler box. Lake water at forty-two degrees. Much vapor in the vicinity of the connecting stream. Looks like a high-rise hot spring.

Today I was ready for a chimney with no flares, curves, or whatever. While it was still frosty, I cut the notch in the rear overhang of the roof to let the chimney through. Slicing through the moss, I found it still eight inches thick and still loose.

I was able to remove the form from the region of the smoke shelf. If a smooth inside to a chimney is important, I have it. Seeing the glassy effect the treatment had done on the arch, I will do likewise with the collapsible form and cover it with plastic.

One more course of stones will put me to the purlin log. About thirty inches to go, depending on how it looks from the lake. One sack of cement left, and a sack has been lasting about two days. I will need another load of sand. Seems I have hauled eight loads so far.

The boss hunter left this afternoon. I heard the sound of his hammer as he boarded up and put a big chain and padlock across the door. A padlock went against the code of old trappers and prospectors, who left a cabin ready for any passerby who needed food and shelter. The lock was there last year, before I came, so perhaps experience has taught him that the cabin code has gone down the drain with a lot of other values.

I watched him take off, and waved. He was too far away for me to see whether he waved back but I like to think he did. I think that about winds up the hunting season for this year. How many rams were taken? How many are left?

■ *September 18th.* Foggy and calm. Twenty-two degrees.

There's a ram stew simmering on the stove with everything in it but the kitchen sponge.

I hauled my last load of sand down from the point and started on the last sack of cement. I hope it will do the remaining twenty-eight inches of chimney. Can't just run down to the corner store out here.

This evening I am just coming out on top of the roof, with about fourteen inches to go. I had to slow down my hot pace to cut flashings out of gas-can tin. By tomorrow evening I had better be done since the cement sack will be empty.

My collapsible form couldn't have worked better. I'm glad I took the time to make it. With it sitting on top of the chimney for the next course, I wondered how the chimney would draw, so I put a piece of scrap tar paper into the firebox and touched it off. The smoke poured up the chimney in fine shape even though the spacers were in the form. When I am finished, I will experiment with the throat to see how much I can close it off and still not smoke up the cabin.

Peppery ram stew for supper. Just the way I like it and plenty of it.

■ *September 19th.* Twenty degrees and clear.

Today I would go as far as I could. The cement would give out by evening. The chimney was taking more mortar than I figured and more time, too. Work was slowing down because of climbing up and down for special-shaped rocks.

About ten-thirty I heard a plane. It was Babe. He had a "brush rat" with him. They had been passing by and just dropped in to check on my progress. He didn't have anything, but he mentioned I had a package. He spread his arms apart to show me how big it was. There was other mail, too. He would be in with it before freeze-up. Most of the lakes down country were already frozen over. Their inspection tour over, off they went, probably to pick up a caribou somewhere.

I have enough cement for one more course of stone. I would have finished, but a man must be polite when company calls.

I took my eggs out of the cooler box and brought them inside. The temperature read thirty-two degrees under the moss. Then I went out to the creek flat on a hunt for special stones for my chimney cap. The fall colors are gone now. Dark brown and grays have replaced the yellows.

Well, the pressure is off! The fireplace is built and what little there is yet to do can be done regardless of the weather. I will allow a few days for curing, and then build a warming fire in the first fireplace at Twin Lakes.

■ *September 20th.* If I was going to stay the winter, I would need more meat. Today was the last day of the sheep season and I liked sheep meat better than caribou. The sight of four good rams in a bunch convinced me.

I put the butchering outfit, camera gear, and musket into the canoe and paddled across the calm lake in the shadow of Crag Mountain. The big rock face of the mountain would hide my approach from the sheep. I decided to leave the camera gear in the canoe. This was serious business today. Up through the spruce and into the high country that I loved, careful not to expose my movements to the sheep. They must know now what a stalking figure on two legs means. I stopped to examine a lone spruce deformed by the wind, a few tufts of branches left near its top. There were fresh tooth marks in the bark and long brown hair hanging from every sliver. The claw marks were higher than I could reach. This was the bears' social register, and the one who had signed it recently was big.

I climbed to a rocky outcrop and eased my head just barely above the rim. There were the rams out of range, lying down and soaking up the sun on a ridge line. I watched until they rose, stretched, took long looks down the mountain, and then trailed off out of sight. I climbed fast. I didn't want them to be out of range next time.

As I peered over the rim where they had been bedded, I saw them again. Closer now, but still out of range—my kind of range, at least. They were on another ridge and climbing slowly. In between was a rocky point and a little saddle. I left my packboard and jacket behind and climbed, keeping the rocks between the sheep and myself. I was breathing hard from the fast scramble and wondered whether I would be able to hit anything when I reached the rocks.

I peeked over the top of a granite boulder. About 200 yards away, the rams were moving behind a grassy knoll. They would appear on the other side of it.

The first legal-curl ram to step into the clear would be my target. I wriggled to some dry grass and waited there on my belly, the safety off the ought-six, my heart thumping against the earth.

Suddenly there he was, a big ram stepping out. A full curl at least. I held the tip of the front sight blade just below the top of his shoulder, took a deep breath, and as I slowly let it out, squeezed the trigger. The shot crashed loud in the high stillness.

I heard the *whunk* of the bullet hitting. The ram did a flip, and down he came sliding and rolling in the new snow. I could see a red spot growing larger on his front shoulder. Down past me he rolled and kept right on going. Maybe he would make it to the timber. I watched him until he stopped. Then I went back for my packboard and pulled on my jacket. My hands were trembling. Up above me three rams posed against the sky for a thrilling moment and dropped out of sight.

My sheep was stone dead. If the bullet hadn't done the job, the fall had. He was a big one, with a little better than full curl and both tips intact. Plenty of meat and a beautiful snowy pelt. I had opened and closed the season in one day, with one shot.

I took him by one heavy horn and dragged him on down the mountain to a level place beneath some spruce trees. As I dressed the big ram out, the camp robbers came gliding in. They perched on the limbs, watching me with inquisitive tilts of their heads as I peeled off the hide. Some ravens croaked from the crags. They had seen the whole show and were talking it over.

At first glance I figured three loads. I took the neck, front quarters, and ribs the first trip. A record trip down to the beach, non-stop. Steady going is the way to do it. Each time you stop to rest, it is harder to go again. One careful step at a time and eventually you're there.

Back up through the timber again to find the camp robbers picking away at the kill. The hind quarters didn't seem too heavy. Maybe I could clean up what was left in one super-load. I had sawed off the skull cap, with horns attached. I put the head, feet, and some other scraps in the hide, which I rolled into a compact bundle. The heart, liver, tenderloin, and brains I put into a flour sack and tucked it between the hindquarters roped on the board. I tied the horns atop the hide bundle. All that was left were the entrails and a few small scraps that the birds and other prowlers of the slopes could share.

It was a much slower trip down the mountain this time. I was glad to get down on the level and see the gleam of the canoe through the brush. It had been a rugged load, but I had saved myself a trip.

Paddling across the still lake, I felt like an Indian hunter returning to a hungry tribe. I glanced up at the high place where I had made the kill. It seemed clouds away.

I put the heart, liver, and brains to soak in a pan. I put the bloody flour sacks, the pelt, and the horns into the lake to soak. I hung the meat in the woodshed for the night, cleaned up all my gear, and put it away.

The pelt must have weighed 100 pounds when I dragged it from the water. Nearly all the blood had soaked out of the white hide, but after I fleshed it I put it back into the lake to finish the job.

Sheep liver and onions for supper. The liver fried two minutes to the side. Pink in the middle, full of flavor, and I ate enough of it. Maybe some of that old boy's ability to romp the high places will rub off on me.

A satisfying day. The search for meat is over. I hate to see the big ram end like this, but I suppose he could have died a lot harder than he did.

▪ *September 21st.* I put my smoker into operation again. I kept it going all day, and while all the meat except the hindquarters cured in the smoke, I worked on the white hide and hung it on two poles to dry in the sun.

Not a pound of meat will be lost due to bullet damage. The bullet hit a whisker high behind the front shoulder. Shooting up at such a steep angle, I should have held a shade lower and would have caught the heart.

▪ *September 22nd.* Smoked the hindquarters today. Salted down the sheep pelt and cleaned up what was left of the skull. The smoked meat of yesterday hung in the woodshed with a plastic covering over it. I found the spruce squirrel tugging at this plastic game bag. Away he bounced over the ground when I yelled at him, and such a fuss from his perch on a branch stub! Stamping his feet and pumping his tail and scolding as if he had more right to the meat than I did.

I hung all the sheep meat high off the ground and covered it with the poncho. I always thought this is the way I would like to do it. Butcher at the right time of the year, hang the meat in the open until it freezes, then just keep sawing off chunks as you need them until it is gone. That's living in the wilderness first class.

■ *September 23rd.* Clear, calm, and a frosty twenty degrees.

Hope Creek is beginning to ice up. I put the thermometer in the creek mouth. Thirty-one degrees. If the creek stopped moving, it would freeze up in no time.

I did a lot of cleaning around the fireplace site today. Picked up all the rocks I didn't use and put them into a single pile away from the cabin. Cleaned up the seams of my last day's work and washed it down. Really looks first-rate.

Now the test for the draft. I took a sprig of fireweed with the seeds ready to fly and shook it in front of the hearth opening. The seed feathers drifted slowly down, then into and up the chimney. I could visually study the flow of air by watching them. Some circulated over the smoke shelf before going on up. This will be a working fireplace, I am sure.

■ *September 24th.* Twenty-five degrees. High, thin overcast.

No pressure now. I might just as well get breakfast in the daylight.

I have decided that rather than put another course of stones on my chimney I will extend the height six inches by making a liner from a gas-can tin. One gas can would do it. I would push it down inside the chimney and insert a few cross ties to make it more rigid.

I was cutting through a seam, which is tough going for a small snips. I was pushing and bearing down hard when it happened. The snips suddenly broke through. My right thumb was sliced open on the back side.

I could move it, so I had missed the tendons, but it was a deep cut just the same. I tied it together with a couple of Band-Aids and wrapped a rag around it. Then I went back to my project. Lucky I didn't have on my good leather gloves which were on the bench beside me. I would probably have cut the right one open, and it wouldn't grow back together as I hope my thumb will do. Soon the addition to the chimney was complete.

No harm in building a small fire under the green chimney, I figured, so I got some shavings and started one. It was satisfying to see the smoke go up and increase in speed as it passed through the throat. Then it started to smoke inside the cabin a bit. I discovered that with the cabin shut tight, air was going up the chimney faster than it was coming in. Opening the window or the top half of the door a whisker corrected the trouble. I am not sure how long I should let the mortar cure before building a normal fire, but I had better wait several days.

About noon I spotted a canoe with two hunters paddling up the far side of the lake through the reflections. In the middle of the canoe was a huge caribou rack, and they were riding low in the water. They must have been thankful for the still water.

I heard a plane leave the lower end. Surely that is the last of the hunters. Tomorrow I will go on a scavenger hunt.

▪ *September 25th.* Thirty-five degrees and overcast. Strange to be free of frost this morning.

Doctored my injured thumb. Washed it thoroughly with soap and warm water and changed the dressing. The slash looks clean. Can't afford any complications. No house calls out here.

I paddled down to the lower end to the remains of the tent camps there. I brought my round-point shovel along.

Why men come into this big clean country and leave it littered the way they do, I will never know. They claim to love the great outdoors but they don't have respect for it. Beer cans, bottles, and cartons were scattered all over the place. Look at the sharp edges of the mountains in the crisp clean air, listen to the creek pouring water you can drink over the stones. Then look around and see all this junk. It's enough to turn a man's stomach. I cleaned up several areas, digging many holes and burying those ugly reminders of thoughtlessness. There were a few rewards, however. I found a big Styrofoam chest with a box of wooden matches inside and some dry soup mix, and collected several empty gas cans. Always a use for them. And finally a bonus, a small roll of haywire.

Seven miles later, on the upper end of the lake, I found the same disregard for the purity of the wilderness. I did my best to erase the ugly scars the visitors had left in their wake.

Must have traveled close to twenty miles today, but it was something I felt I must do. It was payment for the useful items I had found.

■ *September 26th.* Overcast and thirty-eight degrees. Lake water forty degrees, down two degrees from a week ago.

Today I would cut wood to build up my supply. This business of taking wood out of the savings bank and putting none back has been bothering me no end. I filed the one-man crosscut and sharpened the axe to a razor edge with my stone. Then I dropped a few spruce snags. All day long sharp tools ate into wood, and by evening the woodshed had the look of plenty. In its vicinity, beneath the spruce trees and leaning against their trunks, were many logs standing on end, awaiting the saw when the snow deepened.

Plenty of meat hanging from the meat tree, plenty of wood, my cabin tight and warm. I looked forward to freeze-up.

– *Freeze-up* –

■ *November 28th.* Thanksgiving day. Clear, calm, and a minus four degrees. The stars are still out at eight o'clock this morning. The lake is white with frost and in front of the cabin, frozen to a depth of one inch during the night. I could hear the ice groaning on the lower lake, which is shallower and had started to ice over as early as November 2. I hiked along the beach beyond the point to check the upper end of the lake. There was ice along the shore but a big lead of open water beyond Glacier Creek, and a cloud bank of fog was rising where Beaver Creek empties into the upper end.

A special meal today. Fresh suet for the chickadees and a few generous handfuls of meat dust on the stump for the camp robbers and the spruce squirrel. I sawed off loin chops for the main course. The rest of the menu was mashed potatoes and brown gravy, a salad of chopped cabbage, carrots, and onions; sourdough biscuits and honey; sourdough shortcake with fresh blueberries for dessert; and all this washed down with a cup of hot chocolate topped with my last marshmallow. I still had room, so I opened a two-pound tin of cookies that I have been saving since early September. As a result of all this I felt more uncomfortable than I have for a long time.

In preparing for freeze-up, I made a sled out of spruce poles, using the spruce runners I had put in traction. The frame was held together with pegs and short pole bracings. I planed the runners smooth and painted them with a film of wood glue. With its deck poles, handles, and crossbar, it would be a vehicle in which I could push a good-sized load. Too bad I didn't have a pet caribou to pull it.

I mended my snowshoes with the dollar-a-string babiche I had brought in with me. Soaked in warm water for a spell, it became very pliable, and I was able to replace the weakened strings. A fresh coat of shellac and the webs looked ready for miles of trail.

I made a snow shovel out of a fifteen-gallon oil drum Babe had left me. With the wide chisel I cut out the ends, then split the cylinder down the middle. At twenty-two inches around the arc, I split it again. I took some of the curve out of the lower half to give it the proper contact with the ground. For a handle I used twin spruce poles spaced about six inches apart with two crossbars for grips.

From the ends of the drum I made a pair of ice creepers for slick ice and another pair with cleats for climbing in the crusted snow. I accomplished a rough surface on the creepers by driving the point of a spike through the metal in many places. The cleats were three-quarter-inch strips of oil drum folded at the center, and then flattened out a half inch from each end. They were fastened to a metal sole by small sheet-metal screws.

I made an ice chisel out of the wide chisel by fastening it on the end of an eight-foot peeled spruce pole. The pole was augered at the end and split so the chisel handle would lay into it from the side. Then I wrapped it with haywire to make it snug.

Babe had brought me a real glass window that I thought would be a bit of a luxury, but it kept steaming and frosting up and I replaced it with homemade thermopane. This I was able to do by fastening a sheet of thick Mylar plastic (which I got from Sears and which was the mystery package Babe had told me about back in September) with masking tape on each side of the mullions. This left an air space between the two sheets, and the small holes I had bored through the mullions made it really one air space instead of many trapped within the panes.

In the corner of the lower right-hand pane I made a small wooden frame between the Mylar sheets, forming a tiny pane within a pane. Here again a few small holes were bored through the frame to make the air space one. Into this framed compartment I placed a bag of silica gel which absorbed all the moisture between the Mylar layers and kept the window clear. This small pane also had a flap of Mylar over it.

I made some improvements in my fireplace and even installed a fancy damper which brother Jake had sent to me. Many fires had blazed merrily away in the hearth with no smoke at all.

I picked many high-bush cranberries and had made several bottles of syrup for my hotcakes. This gave the maple syrup a rest now and then.

Last week I completed my logging operation on the far side of Hope Creek. I was thinking ahead to the cache project in the spring.

Just yesterday I took my last tour with the canoe. When I beached it, ice was already forming on the metal skin. Now it is stored in Spike's cabin for the winter once more.

Stars and a pale half-moon are rising at four-thirty in the afternoon. The strong wind continues. A fire flickered in the fireplace almost all day. It is good company with its warmth and its wheezing. I like the cast of my big wolf track in its special place atop the log slab mantel.

■ *November 29th*. A thin overcast and a minus two degrees. The wind died during the night.

Chipped through three inches of ice to fill my water bucket a few hundred yards offshore. Yesterday morning I checked the water temperature under the ice. Thirty degrees. No wonder the ice thickens at a rapid rate. Ice as far as I could see up country. In a short time I will have a safe highway for miles in each direction. Freeze-up has arrived.

■ *November 30th*. Dead calm and zero degrees. Frost crystals are building up on the ice. It is like walking on a thick pile rug. The tufts of frost are packed tightly together and over an inch high. The lake ice has increased one inch in twenty-four hours.

The temperature dropped to minus three degrees at noon. I decided to take a trip to the lower end. It's a pleasure to travel the ice. It took one hour to the gravel bank of the connecting stream—not quite as fast as paddling.

I saw big wolf tracks in the drifted snow. They broke through the packed snow where I stayed on top. I saw many more wolf tracks, then a magpie farther down—a bad sign. Blood on the snow. Moose calf tracks, and then about 100 yards farther on, the calf dead on the bank. Blood was frozen on his hind leg above the hock joint. Evidently one of the wolves had hamstrung him while the rest of the pack had held his attention. Had they done it just for sport? Or had they been teaching their young how to go about it? There were smaller tracks in among the larger ones. They had not fed on the carcass at all. Had they actually killed this young bull or did they just disable him and leave him to die? Suddenly the wolves lost a few points with me.

■ *December 1st.* During the night the wind swept the ice free of the frost. I was anxious to be on my way down to the lower end again to check on the calf. If nothing else, it would be meat for my birds and animals.

I tied on my ice creepers and headed down the ice pushing my big sled. The wind drove against my back and squiggles of snow, like frosty snakes, raced over the ice before me.

The long hair on the calf was drifted full of snow, and I soon found that the meat was no good. I could pull hair out by the handfuls and the carcass smelled pretty ripe. I butchered it up into sections, loaded up the sled, and headed for home.

Quite a difference, going against the wind. One gust held me to a standstill. Without my ice creepers I never could have made it. I stowed the meat in the half fifty-gallon drum to freeze, and hung the head in a tree. The magpies soon took command, but there will be plenty for all.

Just before dark I cruised up to my stand on the edge of the log timber. I brushed the snow from a chunk under the spruce and just sat there to think and look and listen. Many sights I had seen there, and many storms. An hour later the temperature took a nose dive and a strong wind started driving snow from down country.

■ *December 2nd.* Minus twenty-two degrees and the continuous complaining sounds of the ice.

I opened up the waterhole. Six and one-half inches—an inch and a half in the last twenty-four hours. Out on the lake, the wind drove the cold right into bones. How many clothes would it take to shut out the cold? Shorts and T-shirt, Frisco jeans and wool shirt vest, red sweatshirt with hood, heavy Navy sweater and insulated coveralls. Then Navy cold-weather wool-lined overalls, watch cap, Navy wool-lined cold weather cap, two pairs of felt inner soles and one pair of cardboard inner soles in my pacs, two pairs of woolen socks, two pairs of woolen mittens, and my heavy woolen scarf. I took a hike up the lake and felt I was dressed about right except I needed more protection for my hands. I came back over the timber trail rather than face a wind that stabbed pain through my cheeks.

Back at the cabin I took a piece of my Glacier Creek ram skin and sewed it into a long tube, hair side in. I fastened a cord to each end so it would hang around my neck. Bare hands shoved into the ends—no wonder those sheep can survive up on the crags!

I filled my kerosene lamp this evening. I made sure the wick was well saturated, then touched a wooden match flame to it. It gives off a soft yellow light and is as quiet as the wilderness, a welcome change from the hissing of the Coleman lantern even though the Coleman throws a whiter, brighter glow. The old kerosene lamp seems to fit into the scheme of things out here—the cabin, the wilderness, and the cold.

I noticed a few air leaks in the cabin. There's frost on the outside of the logs. I plugged up these places with oakum, and I also tacked on more oakum for the door to close against.

■ *December 3rd.* My work on the cabin last evening paid off. It held the heat better last night.

The ice is now eight-and-a-half inches thick at the waterhole, an increase of two inches from yesterday.

It's not too bad working in the woodshed at minus twenty-two degrees. I chopped off a chunk of moose hind quarter. The meat shattered like ice.

Even when they are not feeding, the magpies huddle around the moose head. A chickadee, fluffed to twice his normal size, sat motionless among the spruce needles. There was a ring of frost around his jet bright eye.

■ *December 4th.* Not a breath. Minus thirty-two degrees. The ice groans like a huge wounded animal all through the day. Now that the ice is thicker the sound seems in a different pitch.

Nine-fifteen when Spike's Peak across the lake caught the first rays of the sun.

At minus thirty degrees the moose meat saws like wood. Some prime meat dust for the chickadees, who are puffed up like little gray balloons today and sitting low in the branches to protect those spindly legs. The camp robbers arrived. They looked like giants with their inflated feathers.

While coming back from a trip to the lower end, I saw a movement on the beach, a trotting and a stopping and a trotting again. It was a red fox. He came closer. In this very cold and half-dead world he had smelled the moose meat. How handsome he was in his thick orange coat, black boots, white chest piece, and a white tip on the fat banner of his tail. He came still closer. At fifty feet he started to circle me and not until he crossed my tracks did he get alarmed. Then off he flashed over the ice, his tail flopping this way and that. Abruptly he stopped. He sat on his haunches and studied me.

I put a big chunk of moose meat out on the ice in front of the cabin. Maybe he will come to call by moonlight.

It's very warm in my cabin. At three in the afternoon the shadows are near the tops of the mountains across the lake.

I found it not bad traveling today. The wind is the villain when the thermometer is low. Nature's invisible knife.

■ *December 5th.* A full moon sharply focused in the very clear air. Minus thirty-two degrees. The ice is now twelve inches thick.

Today I would experiment with the cold. Hands and feet are the weaknesses in my protective armor. I cut a pair of insoles from caribou hide. I was sure they would be very effective, but they are too thick with the hair on and make my pacs fit too tight. A thermal insole, a cardboard insole, a thick felt insole, two pairs of woolen socks, one of heavy worsted wool and the other of medium weight, with woolen boot socks seems to be a good combination. A loose fit helps, too. I tried paper between two pairs of socks. It seemed better for a time, then colder. For my hands nothing beats the little "Jon-e" handwarmer fueled with Blazo. Two pairs of woolen mittens with this little handwarmer traded back and forth is surefire protection. I tried paper between two pairs of mittens. That helps, but nothing like the little stove. The Glacier Creek ram skin tube is great protection but a man can't cut wood with his hands shoved into a muff. During these experiments I was working in the woodshed, so I was handy for a quick change of gear.

■ *December 6th.* A yellow pumpkin moon and minus thirty-five degrees.

Good that it is calm. Even a light breeze will make thirty-five below penetrate right into your vitals. By working fast in the woodshed I find I can stay on the comfortable side.

I had another experiment to perform. Protection for my face has been another problem, especially in a wind. A woolen scarf is good for a short while, then it ices up and becomes uncomfortable. I needed something that would stand away from my face and still allow me to see.

A big paper bag might do it. I had not thrown the empty cement sacks away. I shook one out and turned it inside out. Then I cut it in front so it came down to my chest. Next a one-inch slot four inches long to see through. It looked ridiculous, but looks don't count when you're traveling over the ice at thirty-five degrees below zero.

I shoved off for the lower end in my new headgear. It was surprising how warm it was inside my hood. Frosting up a bit, but that was no real problem. I was also wearing a pair of heavy paper mittens between two woolen ones. My hands were fair. Much frost collected on my hood when a breeze hit me. By nearly closing the slot with my stocking cap, I had good protection. A six-mile jaunt round-trip. Next time my little hand warmer goes with me. It is good to know how much cold one can stand and how to dress for it. On taking off my pacs I found my thermal insoles frozen to the soles of the pacs. With the thick felt insoles on top, my feet were warm. I think walking on ice is much colder on the feet than in snow.

■ *December 7th.* Clear, calm, and minus thirty-eight degrees. It seems that below minus thirty-five degrees the air gets hazy as though it is full of tiny frost crystals.

I broke through my waterhole. It was a mass of ice almost immediately.

I was in and out of doors many times today and in my shirtsleeves, too. I must be getting used to this deep freeze.

Strange that I have seen no northern lights yet.

The ice complains less, but when it does, it sounds like a jet plane going by at low altitude. Sometimes it makes a ripping noise as the cracks race through it.

■ *December 8th.* A mild thirty-six below zero. Near sunrise seems to be the low reading.

A good day to check on the mystery trail down the slope of Falls Mountain. I wanted to try out a new device to protect my face, too. I unlaced my Glacier Creek ram skin handwarming tube and made a ruff such as borders a parka hood. Tied the ends together under my chin. With more string I laced the two sides loosely together in the back of my neck. Better visibility than my paper hood.

I crossed the ice to investigate the trail. In the loose snow it was too hard to make out tracks, but I found sheep hair on the brush and many branches broken. I think maybe a lynx attacked the sheep, dragged it down the mountain, then lost its hold, and the sheep escaped. There was no blood on the snow.

It didn't seem like minus thirty-five degrees. I had up a good head of steam going through the spruce timber. Then I saw an odd sight, a small column of vapor rising from the ridgeline.

I had heard bush pilots say that sometimes you can locate a bear in hibernation by the vapor rising from his bunk. I couldn't tell if it was coming from above or below the ridge. I climbed toward it. Sheep tracks and scuff marks exposed grass. Then just above me a few hundred yards I saw three ewes feeding. Their warmth was causing the vapor column that rose perhaps seventy-five feet before it faded out.

Many lynx tracks along the shore of the lake. The cold began to seep in now that I was no longer climbing. Walking with my face down, into a light breeze, the sheepskin was good protection even though a mass of frost collected from much puffing and blowing.

Smoke still coming from the chimney when I returned. A warm forty-five degrees in the cabin.

■ *December 9th.* Minus thirty-four degrees. The ice is quieter now, but once in a while it lets loose with a bellow and sounds like thunder from below.

■ *December 12th.* Plus twenty degrees. Can spring be far away? The ice is now twenty inches thick.

■ *December 13th.* Plus eighteen degrees. T-shirt weather!

I examined the different patterns of cracks in the ice. Some are really impressive and can be seen from top to bottom in the clear ice. It would be interesting to know what the pressure must rise to, to make so much noise and shatter so much ice. The lake has been quiet during this warm spell. About noon today the groaning started again. At times it sounded like the snoring of an army of giants.

■ _December 15th._ Plus twenty-five degrees. Snow driven by a strong wind.

The red fox is a regular visitor now to the moose handout. I believe he will get even tamer as the country gets more hungry.

About eight inches of snow on the level now.

■ _December 16th._ Plus four degrees. Four more inches of snow during the night.

I have a tenant in the john. I heard a racket in there and glimpsed the squirrel flashing over the ridge log. Very soon he was back, his mouth looking like a powder puff. He was carrying moss from the roof. Inside he went, rattled around some, then back out and back in with another load, really working at high speed. While he was gone, I opened the door and looked in. A box of shavings for starting a fire sat just inside the door. It now contained moss as well. He is setting up winter quarters.

■ _December 17th._ Minus nineteen degrees and not a twig stirring. The sun lit the high peaks across the lake at nine-thirty this morning.

Very early this day I felt the cabin begin to shake as if some monster was tossing around beneath it. I heard a low roaring. The lake ice had been noisy, but this sudden earth tremor quieted it for several hours. Along toward daylight I felt another jolting. A look around after sunup convinced me all the mountains were still in their proper places.

That spruce squirrel is working like he has a deadline to meet. A big wad of moss in the shavings box now and a small round hole right in the middle of it.

Wood to saw and split every day. Got to keep up my payments at the Firewood Trust if I want to stay warm this winter. No real problem at all. Some folks had led me to believe it would be an everlasting job—cut wood all day to keep warm all night.

■ _December 19th._ Plus thirty-two degrees. The cold is preferable to a spell like this, with heavy wet snow being dumped from the spruce boughs all through the day.

There is now twenty-three inches of ice.

A bad day for traveling. A good day for little jobs and a chance to catch up on my reading.

■ *December 21st.* Plus four degrees. The shortest day. The sun lighted Allen Mountain across the lake down to the timber line, then dropped out of sight. It will be a pleasure to watch the sun line creep on down to the opposite beach and one day light up my cabin again.

■ *December 22nd.* Wolves on the ice.

I first saw them as little specks close together. Then the leader broke away and the others dropped back to each side to form a wide triangle. They stopped often to turn and look at the stillness surrounding them. Now they came on in a trot. Through the spotting scope I could make out the narrow heads, the erect ears, the long muzzles. I would like to see those green eyes up close. I moved. They froze like statues, 100 yards away. Suddenly one bolted nervously and loped down the ice. The others followed. Too bad I had been in the open when I first saw them. I think I would have gotten a closer look.

■ *December 24th.* Clear, calm, and plus four degrees. I do believe winter at Twin Lakes is better than summer.

Sheep were walking the skyline of the big pasture on Falls Mountain.

I crossed a wolverine track that was headed for Low Pass Creek. I must be on the lookout for that character.

■ *December 25th.* A very white Christmas. No hard feelings toward anyone.

I chopped up some moose meat and scattered these presents for the magpies, the camp robbers, the chickadees, and the squirrel.

Out on the ice I examined a pressure ridge. It was a buckled wall of ice blocks at odd angles about a foot wide and at least four feet high. Some of the slabs of ice had beach rock imbedded in them.

A plane! It was Babe's 180 Cessna. He looked like a skinny Santa Claus as he landed and stepped out with sacks and boxes. He asked how long the lake had been frozen over. Lake Clark had closed up only three days ago.

Lots of mail and grub. Nearly a sack of packages and letters. Six four-pound packages of rice, two large boxes of corn meal, four dozen eggs, plenty of spuds, carrots, lettuce, apples, and celery. Fifty pounds of flour and two slabs of bacon. Cheese, candy bars, and cocoa.

Babe was having roast goose at home so he had to hurry back.

I opened packages and read letters until I had to light the lantern to keep on reading. A Christmas I will never forget. The most no-nonsense Christmas I have ever had.

Babe had given me a time correction. My watch was fifteen minutes fast after no check for four months.

■ *December 27th.* The northern lights last night. No big display. Just a golden glow over the mountains to the northeast. Very much like the breaking of dawn in summer.

It was minus five degrees when I decided to hike down to the lower end. The connecting stream was still open. I saw the bow waves of trout scooting for cover as I walked the bank.

The water ouzels were working as usual, probing the crevices of the stones along the stream edge, then setting sail like miniature ducks, puddling, pirouetting, and disappearing. Moments later, out they came, powder dry and flying into the subzero air with something wriggling in their beaks. They are like big gray waterproof wrens.

Nothing else in sight on the great expanse of snow and ice down country.

The spruce squirrel seems to have a ball of moss for a door. I saw it move when I went to get my fuel to fill the lamp, and out he slipped over the eave log in the rear. I heard him return a few minutes later. In the flashlight beam I saw his "door" was closed. I think he grabs the moss edges at the opening and pulls them together. He will sleep warm tonight even though the temperature is minus ten degrees.

■ *December 28th*. Sheep tracks on the lake. A single sheep had come from the direction of Allen Mountain. Must be a young ram out to see the world. It was the first sheep track I have ever seen on the ice.

■ *December 31st*. Clear, calm, and minus thirty-four degrees.

The squirrel slept in until eleven. I checked his quarters and his moss ball door was closed, almost as if he had put out a sign, do not disturb.

Where do the birds go in these low temperatures?

When I opened the door, a cloud of vapor would rush in through the lower half and roll to the fireplace. Then a cloud would rush out the top half and cover the overhang of the roof with frost.

Thirty-two degrees below zero during the heat of the day.

I sawed up a log to restore the dent I was putting in my wood supply. I wrapped the saw handle with paper and my hand didn't get too cold.

Toward evening I hiked a couple of miles down the lake. I was dressed in two sweaters, shirt vest, insulated coveralls, stocking cap and Navy foul weather cap, wool gloves and lined buckskin mittens, heavy Navy scarf, and my sheepskin hood. I found the hip pockets of my coveralls good protection for my mittened hands. It was minus thirty-six degrees when I returned to the cabin, my hood a mass of frost.

For my waterhole I had cut a six-inch chunk from a big log and set it over the hole, filling around it with snow. No more than a half-inch of ice had formed under it. That saves a lot of chipping.

■ *January 2nd*. Forty-five below. A land without motion. In the dead of winter nothing seems to move, not even a twig on the willows.

The thickness of the ice is now a strong twenty-eight inches. In this very cold weather the hole in the ice gradually closes in from the sides until it is a hole no longer.

A pan of hot water tossed into the forty-five-below air turns to a cloud of steam with a loud hissing noise.

■ *January 3rd.* Doldrum-still and minus forty-five degrees.

Today I would go up the canyon to Low Pass 1,600 feet above the lake to see what problems a man would have to face at this temperature.

What did I learn from my four-hour round trip? With no wind I could travel all day in minus-forty five-degree cold and be comfortable. A few mountains in the way might help. If a man carried an axe, it would be no problem to camp in thick timber, dry out, and sleep warm in a down sleeping bag. On such a trip snowshoes are a must, and climbers would be needed on the hard mountain crust.

Brush breaks in the extreme cold as if dry and dead.

It is warmer on top of the pass than it is along the lake. Moisture must make the difference. My face and fingers felt the bite of the cold as soon as I reached lake level.

I found frost from top to bottom between my outside and second layer of clothing. My pacs had snow inside to the tip of the toes, and I was covered with frost. I had a heavy feeling in my chest and wondered if I had hauled too much of that forty-five-below air into my lungs.

■ *January 7th.* Plus seven degrees and calm. A half inch of fluffy snow fell during the night.

More fox tracks than I have ever seen. I think my moose bait is beginning to bring out the hungry ones.

I hiked down to the connecting stream. It was still open. I doubt it will ice over this winter. The trees and brush along its banks are feathered with frost from the vapor rising from the open water. Tracks and a slide announced that an otter had traveled the stream. Run and slide, run and slide. He slides a great distance after only a step or two.

No sign of caribou or any other game.

■ *January 9th.* What do you know? Here comes Babe in the T-Craft on skis, his exhaust stacks streaming out two vapor trails!

"Cold down here," he greeted. It was thirty-five below. "Lots warmer up high."

He brought a burlap sack half full of butter beans, fifty pounds of sugar, four ten-pound sacks of fine graham flour, a big box of dried apples, six boxes of raisins, and five boxes of pitted dates. Also some mail.

No hurry today. He sat and talked and watched my fresh kettle of beans cooking. Yes, this is what he would enjoy—living out like this in a cabin if he didn't have so much responsibility that the Lord had heaped upon him. He felt it was his duty to talk to people and spread His word. A man could hardly do that living in a cabin.

"Say," he asked suddenly, "do you suppose those beans are done yet?" He ate two bowls full and allowed they were pretty good beans.

We had covered the T-Craft engine to hold the heat, and it started first flip of the prop. He has a heater now, a catalyst-type gas heater sitting on the floor. Also has his engine heater handy, too. The old boy hasn't lived all these years in the Far North for nothing.

Next trip, he said, he might bring the mission girls along to see the cabin. I watched him zip over the crust and draw away, trailing a short stream of vapor.

The ice is now thirty-two inches thick.

As I stored some of my provisions away in Spike's cabin, I thought about the cache I would build come spring.

Babe also had brought me two pairs of heavy socks that his wife had knitted for me. And another surprise, a detachable parka hood quilted with feathers between the layers, and a ruff of wolfskin around the face.

■ *January 12th.* Minus thirty-six degrees.

I crossed the lake to see the sun. It was really a thrill to see my shadow again, but I could feel very little warmth. The pale golden light flooded the ice for about 100 yards from the far shore, then faded into shadow once more as the sun winked out of sight behind the shoulder of Gold Mountain.

■ *January 14th.* A sliver of a moon and minus sixteen degrees.

My first trip on snowshoes. It was good to hear the soft crunch of the crust beneath the webs as I slung along the creek trail. It had been tough going on previous days without snowshoes. I enjoyed looking back in the sharp air at my tracks winding through the white stillness. Very little game spotted. Two sheep, but just because you don't see game, that doesn't mean it isn't there. Today's bonus was the exhilaration of the trip itself.

■ *January 15th.* Warmer weather with the dark of the moon. Minus eight degrees.

I had seen no moose in the cottonwoods across the lake since the low slopes had been in shadow, and I wondered if the coming of the sunlight to those levels would signal a return of the big animals.

There were dark objects in the cottonwoods. Moose! Welcome back! I snowshoed up along the brush to get a better look. A huge bull with a majestic rack, a cow, and a young bull with antlers like a buck deer. They moved as they browsed, and when they stopped it was invariably behind brush or a tree. They moved not in alarm but warily, not affording me a view in the clear. In their slow passage they flushed ptarmigan, and the birds croaked their irritation as they scaled away to land farther on.

The ice is now thirty-five inches thick.

■ *January 17th.* Plus ten degrees.

I am having a creosote problem. Too much low fire in the stove. Creosote runs down the stovepipe from each joint. Some of it is even running down on the roof and getting through to my logs.

■ *January 18th.* Almost like summer. A plus twenty-two degrees.

A good day to try to solve the creosote problem. I let the fire go out and took down the stovepipe. Then I relocated the damper and put the pipe back, bottom end up. Now the joints in the pipe lead in instead of out. Can't be any worse than it was. Time will tell.

▪ *January 20th.* Plus two degrees.

Field day. I scoured my table and counter top with Comet powder, soap, and bleach. With Babe always threatening to bring the mission girls next trip, I had better keep this place shipshape.

My stovepipe has been staying clean. No strong odor when I build up my fire for cooking. That's a good sign.

I saw the squirrel today. He has been making himself scarce. I thought a fox got him, or maybe the weasel, but the little troublemaker is back.

A slice of moon this evening. As that moon becomes full, the temperature will drop like a stone or I miss my guess.

▪ *January 22nd.* Three and a half inches of fluffy snow. Plus fifteen degrees.

I made a snowshoe trail down country. When I returned later on the same trail, I found it all but drifted shut. I had a tendency to wander off course in the surrounding whiteness. Far out from shore I came across the trail of a mouse. I think he must have thought that this is a big world.

The fox, the magpies, and some ravens were around the moose meat. They must have an understanding with each other. Sometimes the fox chases the magpies, but it seems more in play than anything else.

Three big rams were above Glacier Creek, standing up to their bellies in the snow. Bare places show where they had foraged for grass.

▪ *January 31st.* Snowing. Plus eighteen degrees.

Twenty-eight inches of snow on the level and as loose as feathers. January has not been the cold month I expected it to be. What will February bring?

▪ *February 1st.* Fog and snowing lightly. Minus two degrees.

I snowshoed a narrow flight strip for Babe. It is good to have something by which to judge distance and the condition of the snow. This will be the Twin Lakes International Airport.

A small flock of sparrow-sized birds have come in like a flurry of dry leaves to land and feed on the tips of the buckbrush. They show a rosy color. My field guide pictures them as hoary redpolls.

■ *February 3rd.* Clear, calm, and thank the Lord! Forty-eight degrees below zero. That full moon has brought another chill to this land.

It was a happy sight to see my cabin bathed in sunlight for one-half hour today.

I was sawing wood when I heard a plane. The little Black Bird from Lake Clark. Babe was putting out a longer vapor trail than the last time he came. He made a circle and came in to light on my packed strip. He had trouble taxiing because the aluminum skis had a tendency to stick to the snow.

"Man, it's cold here!" he exclaimed, beating his mittened hands together. He bounced around in his wolfskin coat and sheepskin pants. He seemed to be causing his own fog bank.

"Can't stay long or I'll be part of the scenery," he said. He was afraid the oil would freeze at this low temperature. Lots of mail and packages. Two more pairs of very heavy woolen socks that Mary Alsworth had knitted. They're so pretty I hate to think of wearing them. And three big bags of popping corn.

But where were the mission girls? Next time he would bring them for sure.

I broke him loose from the snow and held a wing until he was turned around. Away he went, anxious to climb a few thousand feet to where it was warm.

I thawed a bowl of blueberries, bruised them up a bit for more juice, added some white sugar and syrup, and enjoyed a treat to celebrate the return of the sun.

■ *February 4th.* Minus fifty-one degrees. Clear and cemetery-still.

I find that it is as much as two degrees colder down on the lake than at the cabin, and there is only a difference of four feet in elevation.

I was eager to try a pair of my new heavy socks, along with a pair of insoles in my pacs, one pair of light wool socks, and the heavy ones over them. It was fifty below zero as I followed the trail up the hump, and thirty below on top.

Those sixteen-inch heavy socks with their close knit really kept my feet warm or else I'm getting used to the frost.

Within a few days there will be an hour of sunlight at the cabin.

■ *February 5th.* Minus forty-eight degrees.

When I turned in at ten o'clock last night, it was fifty-four below zero. Now the moon is past the full. I think this will be the record low temperature for the winter.

At these low temperatures my binoculars frost up so quickly that I can use them for only a few seconds at a time.

The camp robbers were here, with streaks of frost back from their eyes. They didn't appear very hungry, just disinterested balls of feathers decorating the spruce boughs. The magpie deserves a lot of credit. Robber that he is, he really works at making a living. He sits there and pecks away at that frozen moose meat in the fifty-below.

Snow blowing from the peaks and ridges. In a very short time some of the high places lost their solid whiteness. That should make the sheep happy. Feed is being uncovered up there.

I snowshoed across the lake to investigate a track below the rock face. There was a sun dog on either side of the sun as the overcast darkened. Trailing up through the deep snow, I was showered by more snow from the spruce. As soft and loose as the snow is, a snowshoe rabbit sinks in only about three inches. I startled a flock of spruce grouse and they exploded, knocking snow from the limbs in their panic. A few minutes later I struck the trail of a lynx. He sank deep and dragged his big feet toward the rock face. He had made those mystery tracks.

My trail to the cabin was all but drifted shut in the wind and driving snow, but the thermometer back at the cabin read plus ten. The cold spell is broken.

■ *February 6th.* Plus eighteen degrees. Quite a variation in twenty-four hours, from minus forty-eight to plus eighteen.

The wind is roaring across the peaks. Snow is streaming from them like smoke from a grass fire. The thickness of the ice is now thirty-six inches, and the temperature of the water is thirty-one degrees.

I nailed the forked roots of a spruce stump on the end of the ridge log above the door. I call it the spruce buck. It will make a good perch for the birds.

I had to break out another jar of oatmeal. Surely I must hold a record for consuming the largest quantity of rolled oats in a few month's time.

■ _February 12th._ A strong breeze and plus twenty-five degrees.

Today I would carve a big wooden spoon for Mary Alsworth in exchange for the heavy boot socks. I dug out a likely piece of stump stock from the deep snow and went to work. She wanted a spoon with lots of curve so that is the way it would be. While I worked, the camp robbers kept me company. When they come a-begging, I always have time to feed them. They seem to have found the spruce buck perch to their liking. A kettle of beans simmered away on the fire, and when they were done, so was the spoon.

The break in the cold gave my windows a chance to shed their buildup of ice today. Good to have them clean and dry again.

■ _February 13th._ Snowing. From down the lake a strong wind is blowing big flakes. Plus thirty degrees.

When the lake is open, you do not hear the wind in the mountains. Today the sound of it was like the roaring of a great waterfall.

■ _February 14th._ The heat wave continues. Plus thirty degrees.

An old visitor in his winter overcoat came to call today, his slender body doubling and stretching as he bounced over the snow. Out of respect for his new robe, I will call him an ermine instead of a weasel.

I think I know where the squirrel went. The ermine must have killed him. I saw the ermine snake into the squirrel's nest.

A camp robber was inside the cabin. When I came through the door, he flew to the bunk post. I approached him. He didn't fly. I picked him up and he struggled a bit in my hand. I held a meat scrap in front of him. First he pecked at my finger and then at the meat. For a moment he sat there in the palm of my hand. Then with a sudden takeoff he flew out the door to a spruce branch, where he sat very quietly as if puzzled by the experience.

■ *February 15th.* Clear and calm and plus six degrees.

A camp robber swooped inside and grabbed up a meat scrap while his two companions hesitated on the spruce buck. Those characters must have been talking things over.

The ermine has taken over the squirrel's quarters. He left as I opened the door, then returned cautiously, climbed back into the box, crawled into the nest, reached out to get a mouthful of moss, and closed his door. I tempted him with a meat scrap. A little wary at first, but his belly got the best of him. He latched on to the opposite end of the scrap, and when I didn't let go with his tugging, he came right on up and went for my fingers. He's not one to back into a corner. There's a tiger in that little body.

■ *February 21st.* Plus twenty-six degrees. Snowing and blowing.

Twenty-seven inches of snow on the level. My snow shovel works well. My paths are beginning to look like small canyons with steep white walls.

It's a good thing that a weasel is not the size of a fox. He is a powerhouse for his size. The little ermine's body can't be more than ten inches long, yet he can wrestle a meat scrap that weighs several pounds. I saw him flashing in and out beneath the mortar tub where the moose meat was stored. Such a racket! Every now and then he would bolt right up straight and look around to see if he was attracting attention. The magpies give him a lot of room. He could easily kill one, and they don't give him a chance to prove it. He is compact savagery. The way he moves he must have voltage in his veins instead of blood.

I snowshoed the airstrip down and outlined it with small spruce boughs. Not really necessary, but the roughing up of the surface and the boughs help a pilot's depth perception.

■ *February 23rd.* Minus sixteen degrees.

I was halfway down the lake when I heard a plane. Sure enough, it was the little Black Bird. Babe made two circles coming down and scooted in on my airstrip. I reached him just as he unpacked the last item. We turned the plane around facing the sun and covered the engine. He was in no hurry today.

"You know when I left here in the cold last time," he said, "I had oil temperature but no oil pressure until I climbed up high. Man, you live in a deep freeze!"

All kinds of mail and packages. Some extra warm mittens and mukluks from brother Jake. Two small bags of nuts with a tag, stale nuts for squirrels.

Right away I remembered a story Hope Carrithers liked to tell. A little boy was watching another little boy eat a big red apple. "Can I have the core?" he asked. The other boy answered, "Ain't gonna be no core." That is what I will tell the squirrels. They can't read, and they don't know nuts are for squirrels anyway.

A new pair of Eddie Bauer shoe pacs from Spike. Cookies from home. Some special peanut brittle. My order from Sears, which included some new stovepipe. And last but not least, a big package from brother Jake—a cast-iron log rack for my fireplace.

I popped some corn and broke out the can of peanut brittle. We swapped yarns and I worked on my outgoing mail while Babe lowered the can of peanut brittle.

"Only that much," he grinned, holding his thumb and forefinger about three inches apart. He said Mary would be tickled with the big wooden spoon, the stirring spoon, and the fork I had made for her.

"That is a pretty little strip from the air," he said, "and them spruce tips make the landing easier."

On the first flip of the prop the T-Craft engine started. "May bring the mission girls next trip," he shouted, and off he whirred, climbing fast toward the ridge.

I looked at my fancy mittens and mukluks. The challenge of keeping warm at Twin Lakes is gone even though the temperature may drop to seventy below. These hand and foot coverings have plugged the weakness in my protection.

I don't know why I waste time worrying about the squirrel. He'll probably die of old age. I saw him bounce across the woodshed roof today. He must have been smart enough to move out just ahead of the weasel moving in.

Somehow I never seem to tire of just standing and looking down the lake or up at the mountains in the evening even if it is cold. If this is the way folks feel inside a church, I can understand why they go.

I wish brother Jake could be here to see the red logs glowing on the cast-iron rack.

■ *February 27th.* Plus twenty-six degrees and driving snow.

While the kettle of lima beans was bubbling on the fire, I opened my tin-bending shop. I made some covers out of gas cans for my pans.

I noticed that a piece of moose meat I had put out for the magpies was gone. While working in the woodshed, I heard a sharp little bark. It was the weasel in the woodpile trying to scare me away from the moose meat he had dragged there. Many times he barked, stabbing his head out from different places in the jumble of split spruce. When I left, there he was, sitting upright like a fence picket.

■ *February 28th.* No wind. Plus twenty-eight degrees and overcast.

February gone. That didn't take long. Still the snow depth stays at twenty-seven inches at my checking station. It settles between snows.

■ *March 2nd.* Plus eighteen degrees. With a full moon, I don't understand why it continues so mild.

Last night before turning in, I went out on the ice to cover the water hole and check the baited hook I had left dangling just off the bottom. The line pulled heavy with throbbing tugs. The gas lantern lighted the water to the bottom of the ice three feet down, and beyond. The fish was struggling down there, eyes aglow, a pale lake trout, fins and tail nearly white and the spots on its sides barely visible. It was icy to the touch as I flopped it out on the snow.

I was anxious to see what the trout measured so I hurried to the cabin. A good sixteen inches. I spilled water into my dish pan and put the fish into it. It struggled to swim, trying to turn end for end. I decided that a beautiful trout like this belonged sixty feet down in the clear, cold water of the lake. I couldn't see it browning in the skillet.

Gently I slipped the trout through the thin skin of ice covering most of the waterhole. Around and around it swam, attracted to the bright light. I left, and when I returned a while later it was gone. No doubt as the trout descended once more into the blackness, it felt as if it had been to the moon and back.

The snow was in good shape for a trip and the weather was fairing up, so off I went on the webs, down the lake. I could barely see the weave of my last snowshoe trail, and it was important that I follow it. Save the effort of breaking a new trail in the deep snow. I soon came upon the tracks of a wolverine crossing from Low Pass Creek over to Emerson Creek. That animal covers a lot of miles. No doubt it had come from the valley of the Kigik.

I found some caribou, too. They were in single file crossing a slide of loose rock that the winds had blown bare. Very few antlers in the bunch. One of them had only one antler. I saw him shake his head as if trying to get rid of it.

The connecting stream was nearly closed. This was surprising when it was wide open at fifty below. It must have been the big wind after the last snow that did it. The water was cold enough to freeze, and did when wind blown snow choked the flow.

Two sheep were etched sharply on a crag against a salmon-colored sunset.

My birds greeted me when I returned. One took a meat scrap out of my hand, then pecked me on the finger as much as to say, "Who's afraid?"

■ _March 3rd._ Overcast and plus twenty-seven degrees. Snow curling from the peaks like smoke.

Sunlight bathing my cabin at ten-fifteen. This had not happened in several months. There was that big golden ball breaking through the overcast, high enough to shine through the deep gunsight notch on the shoulder of Cowgill

Peak. Soon it winked out again behind the slant of boulders. At twelve-ten it came out again just below the peak. A few more days and there will be sunshine on the logs from ten o'clock to five-thirty.

Tonight the full moon is trying to find holes in the cloud cover.

■ *March 4th*. Plus twenty-four degrees.

A trip up the lake on this very clear day. Rocks rattling down the mountains now and then were the first hints of spring. I glassed the slopes for bear tracks but saw none. A fresh wolverine track was headed my way. Running his circuit probably on both sides of me. Maybe I will catch sight of him yet. Very warm in the sun but cool in the shadow of the mountain as I snowshoed back to the cabin.

A stranger was perched near the top of a spruce. Gray and round headed, big yellow eyes—a hawk owl. He dropped silently from his lookout, and in a long swoop, glided up country with a camp robber in hot pursuit.

■ *March 5th*. Plus twenty-six degrees.

The track of the wolverine again, this time behind the cabin at the foot of the hump in the spruce timber. Headed up country in his usual sidewise lope. I followed him for a spell. Here he would slow to a walk to investigate beneath low hanging branches or a blowdown, and then off again on the trot. He makes his living on what others leave behind. He leaves his sign but I never see this phantom of the wilderness.

A strong wind makes this evening a good one to appreciate my shelter.

■ *March 10th*. Plus thirty-two degrees. This weather will mess around until it is too late to get cold again until next winter.

I was washing dishes when I heard a warbling call, like a cabin robber but much louder. It was a bird I had never seen before, light gray over all, with darker back and tail. A black strip ran from the base of its slightly curved beak right through its eye like a mask. My bird book says it's a Northwestern shrike.

Easy pickings for the sheep now, as much of the big pasture is free of snow.

The sound of a plane interrupted my wood splitting. Slipping into Twin Lakes International Airport was the little black plane. I hadn't expected Babe for a week, and my clean-up of the cabin not complete!

Where were the mission girls? He would bring them next trip. Lots of mail and packages.

Brother Jake must come up here and help me eat these groceries he sends. Here's a box of Band-Aids in case I tangle with a bear. Some burn ointment for the bright days ahead. And a bottle of aspirins for a broken leg. How about that?

I finished my outgoing mail about the same time Babe finished the popcorn. Nice weather down at Lake Clark. The rivers were opening up. Airfield at Iliamna in bad shape and no mail from there in a week.

Babe was thinking seriously of building a log chicken house. From the number of questions about logs and putting them together, I suspect all I have to do is hint and I would have a job.

Babe reminded me that caribou season closes March 31st. When he came again, we might look for one.

I gave him clearance for takeoff, and off he went in a swirl of snow.

With all this gear I have been accumulating, that cache is a must. Spike's cabin can't take much more.

I heard a fly buzzing around. It landed on a log to soak up the sun. I hung the thermometer next to it. The mercury stopped climbing at seventy-six degrees. In the shade it read forty-two degrees.

I mended my snowshoes. They really needed attention. Wet snow ruins the webs in no time.

■ *March 11th.* Plus fifteen degrees.

I am lakebound until my snowshoe webbings dry tight as a drum head. It is impossible to travel in the brush without them. I have given the webs a coating of polyurethane.

A good day to catch up on the woodpile.

■ *March 12th.* Plus twenty-three degrees. Another few inches of snow during the night.

I have been curious to see how much ice there is on the lower lake. Packing my ice chisel and shovel, I headed for my experimental area. The top six inches of the lake ice seem to be the hardest. Farther down I made good time. Forty-four inches when I broke through. Eight inches more than the upper lake. Satisfied with what I had learned, I headed back to the cabin for lima beans and sourdough biscuits.

■ *March 13th.* Plus sixteen. Snowing.

Today was the day to give that fancy can of Sears polyurethane varnish a workout. I kept the fireplace going and the door open for good ventilation. Everything that could take varnish got the full treatment—the counter, the table, the shelves, the window ledges, the wash bench. They all took on a shiny look. By midafternoon everything was dry, and I put things back where they belonged. Let those mission girls come now!

The lake is beginning to complain again after a long quiet spell.

■ *March 15th.* Clear, calm, and minus twenty-eight degrees. Spring five days away, but this country doesn't know it.

A good day to try out my G.I. mukluks and mittens. Nothing spectacular appeared during my trip along the slopes. No big game at all, a few spruce grouse and some ptarmigan. I saw the tracks of a lynx and porcupine tracks in the big cottonwood grove. I can do without porcupines. Their teeth ruin the handles of tools left in the wrong places.

The connecting stream is now open end to end.

I must give the mukluks and the mittens a high performance rating.

■ *March 16th.* Clear and calm. Minus twenty-two degrees. A veil of overcast is robbing the sun of its power.

Last night at ten o'clock I saw streaks in the night sky to the north and the northeast. I put on my cold-weather clothes and went out on the ice to watch the show. It was the best I have seen. A weaving curtain of green hung over the Glacier Creek country, spreading large one moment and shrinking small the next. Streaks of red, yellow, and green shot like searchlight beams to a point overhead. Clouds of colored light like brilliant fog patches blinked on and off. All alone in the subzero cold, with the heavens on fire and the ice cracking and crashing around me. A savage scene, and one to remember.

■ *March 19th*. Plus twenty-seven degrees. Dancing flakes of snow beneath a gray sky.

I accomplished something today. At last all the camp robbers will take scraps from my fingers. Today the old veteran with the spots on his head decided to get into the act. He had been watching his two companions from his perch on the spruce-buck horns just above my head. His mind and body seemed willing to take the plunge toward the scrap I held out to him, but his feet wouldn't let go of the perch. He gyrated and nearly lost his balance. Finally he dropped to my hand for a split second and left in panic with the meat scrap. It will be easier next time.

The waterhole isn't closing in as fast as before. The ice-making season is just about over.

On one of my trips I had noticed a huge burl on a dead spruce tree. Today I would go back and salvage it. A king-sized one it was, measuring thirty inches by twenty-seven inches and about fourteen inches thick. I slabbed it with a four-inch cut next to the tree, then a three-inch cut. The cap would be about seven inches deep, and perhaps from that I could carve a bowl. Plenty of sawing, and while I sawed, the wind picked up. By one-thirty in the afternoon I was finished.

Two slabs on the packboard and in for lunch. Back again for the cap and the tools. Now the wind was howling and wailing through the boughs.

I removed the bark from my prize burl sections with the sharp block plane. The slabs will make interesting table tops. While I worked in the woodshed, the three camp robbers came begging, and I had to get some meat scraps for them. They get so excited they can hardly wait their turn to come to my hand—sometimes two at once.

To celebrate the first day of spring tomorrow, I will take a jar of blueberries from my underground cooler box.

■ *March 24th.* Dense fog and a plus four degrees.

A fox misses very little in his prowlings among the snow drifts. One has been in and out the brush near the big chunk of moose meat bait, and he knows exactly what he is doing. He watches the magpies as they whack away at the frozen meat with their bills. They hop away with hard-earned morsels and bury them in the snow. Back they come, beaks white to the eyes, to peck and twist away some more. And the fox patiently waits to make his rounds of their storage places, to gulp the bite-size pieces. Maybe that's what the conversation of the magpies is all about when they find out what the red pirate has done.

The ptarmigan are talking on the slopes. Their voices sound like the croaking of frogs.

■ *March 26th.* Plus twenty-four degrees. An inch of snow as dry as powder during the night.

A good day to check the snow register and see who signed in recently. I was about a mile up the lake when the sound of a plane pulled me up short. It was Babe all right. Had he brought the mission girls this time?

When I reached the cabin, Babe was unloading a front quarter of caribou. He had brought his rifle along. There were thousands of caribou just beyond the mountains. He had landed on a small lake, where caribou were all around. He had butchered three—the limit—dressed them out to cool, and came on up here hoping the day would get colder and the snow better for takeoff with a heavy load.

I told him I had plenty of meat left and must get it used up before warm weather. Others at Port Alsworth could use it more than I, so we loaded the shoulder into the little Black Bird again. He hadn't expected to be out this way, so the mission girls were still back at the mission. He stayed for a short while, then he started thinking about something getting to the caribou before he did, and off he went.

The sun was warm and the eaves dripped. A bald eagle soared past. I wonder if he spotted the moose bait?

• *March 27th.* Plus five degrees. The sky not as blue as it should be. Looks like the weather is about to change.

I went down to the lower end of the lower lake to check on the caribou and see if their new antlers were showing yet.

I crossed the trail of two wolves traveling side by side. They looked as though they were headed for sheep country. Do they change their menu now and then? Babe says they prefer moose to caribou.

From the mouth of a canyon I glassed down country and found a big spread of caribou about three miles below the lower end of the lake. I spotted another bunch closer, and they told me what I wanted to know. Most had no antlers at all, but a few showed knobby stubs about three inches long.

It was getting late. It would take three hours of steady going to get back home, against a breeze that chased the powder snow over the crust.

There were big tracks near the magpie bait when I returned. A pigeon-toed walk and toes spread out wide—the wolverine. Not a bit bashful, he had nosed around the barrel with the moose meat in it. Tomorrow I will track him.

Before I went to bed I dropped a heavy chunk of moose meat into the snow.

• *March 28th.* Cloudy and plus twenty-five degrees.

It seemed as though I had no more than turned in last night when it was daylight. I looked out. The moose chunk was gone.

After breakfast I followed the fresh trail going toward Hope Creek. A few moose hairs on the snow told me I was on the right track. Across the creek it wound, into the brush headed toward Cowgill Creek. Not once had the wolverine set the load in the snow. Finally in a gully I saw a blood-stained patch on the packed snow, and a chunk of bone. A bit farther he had stopped to eat again. The magpies were helping. They were ahead of me, picking up crumbs at the third feeding place.

I found two beds in the snow and a fresh track leading on. The wolverine climbed higher as he headed down country. I probably had been discovered. He had stopped now and then on a high place to look back over his trail.

At a point with a good command up and down the lake, I took a stand and studied my surroundings with the binoculars. Nine head of sheep were up on the edge of the big pasture. Then I saw something on the ice, about halfway out. The wolverine was crossing to the far side. Through the lenses I could see the cream-colored stripes on his dark back, that rocking-horse gait as he loped, stopping often to look back. He climbed the bank of the far side. One last look back, then he disappeared into the timber.

I spent the afternoon fattening up the woodpile. In the evening I took more moose meat out of the barrel and tied it to the front end of the sled. As the meat goes, so goes the sled. My cabin is where the action is these days.

■ *March 29th.* I wonder if this morning's minus-one will be the last below-zero reading this spring?

The sled and moose bait were as I left it last evening. I found fresh wolverine tracks on the point up the lake from the cabin. He came back, but he was circling as if suspicious of a handout.

All through the day I heard the thump of falling rocks, and now and then a rolling roar that signaled a snow slide. I watched snow pouring over the ledges of Crag Mountain, like water over a falls.

The sun sets one diameter higher on the slope of Falls Mountain. In a month it will be dropping behind the peak.

■ *March 31st.* Foggy. A fine snow drifting down at plus twenty-five degrees.

What a surprise when I looked out! My sled was pulled up against the willow brush on the point a good thirty feet from where I had left it. The skunk bear had returned in the night.

After breakfast I went to investigate. Tracks and the brushing strokes of a broad tail showed much bracing of feet, pulling, and yanking. It had been upgrade all the way. The snow was packed and soiled with blood at the end of the rope. He cleaned up everything, or took what was left. I had tied the rope around the moose hindquarter and the loop was still on the rope end. What I need is a silent alarm system to wake me while the raid is in progress.

That evening I heard suspicious sounds. I rushed out with my flashlight and there was the wolverine about 200 feet out on the ice, his eyes blazing in the beam. He didn't seem in any particular hurry as he ambled toward Hope Creek flats, stopping often to stare at me. An animal of about thirty pounds or more, with the combined mannerisms of a skunk and a small bear.

I would be ready if he came again in the night. I roped some more moose meat to the sled and parked it on the ice out from the waterhole. From the sled I ran a long cord up the path to the cabin and through the kitchen window.

When I turned in for the night, I wrapped a couple of turns of the cord around my wrist. If the wolverine took off with the sled, I would not be far behind.

▪ *April 1st.* Foggy. Plus twenty-two degrees.

I really couldn't sleep last night thinking about the wolverine. At ten-thirty in the dark cabin I rested my elbows on the counter and peered out on the moonlit apron of the lake. It was a little before midnight when he came, around the point of willow brush along my snowshoe trail to where the bait had been the day before.

He loped a few steps, then stopped with head low as if listening, advanced in a rippling motion, stopped again. Suddenly he "chickened out" and retreated, but spun around to advance again. He repeated this performance several times until his appetite overruled his judgment.

He jerked savagely at the bait. The line tightened. The sled didn't budge. The runners were frozen fast to the ice. He decided to eat right there and I watched him working over the bait.

I had fresh batteries in my flashlight. I eased the window to a more open position, laid the barrel of the flashlight flat on the ledge and flicked on the switch. His eyes sparkled like big blue diamonds in the bright swath at one 100 feet.

Then he did a strange thing. He went back to his eating as if the light was nothing unusual at all. He fed gluttonously, looked at the light, then turned his back to it. A few minutes later he loped away fifty feet or more, only to return and feed again. I studied his beautiful pelt, all powdered with snow, in the glare of the light until he finally left with a heavy belly.

This morning I was awake at five. Just as I unwrapped the alarm cord from my wrist, it went hissing over the window ledge. I jumped out of the bunk and saw the wolverine at the bait. There was some slack in the meat line attached to the sled, so he had picked up the meat and headed off down the lake when the line attached to the sled brought him up short.

The sound of the cord running out over the window ledge spooked him, and he probably heard me stirring around, too. After many starts and stops to look back, he headed up the lake, then veered into the brush.

Later on I found his tracks all over the place. He is definitely a trail traveler. Every time he hits one of my snowshoe trails, he follows it wherever it winds. He even runs his own tracks a second time.

Strangely, although his tracks are all around my mortar-mixing tub bottom-side-up over the meat barrel, he made no effort to get the moose quarter beneath it. A very light push would tip off the tub and expose the meat.

He must know it is the ermine's territory. If an ermine weighed thirty-five pounds too, he would have a wolverine for breakfast every morning.

I cut a hole in the ice 200 yards out where the snow cover is kept shallow by the wind. The ice was forty-three inches thick over 280 feet of water.

■ *April 4th.* Clear and calm. Minus two degrees.

I was awakened last night with a yank. The line flew off my wrist, and the spool to which the line was attached skittered over the gravel floor. I snubbed up and stopped whoever was pulling on the other end. He had turned the sled and was pulling it down country. He went about fifty feet before I stopped him.

Then started the tug of war. I hauled the meat chunk my way, him right on top of it with his front paws, his head shaking from side to side as he tore at the hide and muscle of the leg bone. I pulled him my way until the sled stopped me because it had turned crosswise. Then I would give him line and he would pull it smoking over the snow.

I snubbed the line to a shelf bracket and set up my spotting scope. With the aid of the flashlight, I got a close look. There he was, the king of the weasel family, with short, rounded ears, teeth bared and glistening, muzzle wrinkled like an angry chow, eyes blazing blue—a sight to remember. Abruptly he quit the struggle and loped out into the blackness.

I followed his tracks this morning. I found he had bedded down under a small spruce where the needles were dry. I had interrupted his sleep, as was revealed by fresh tracks up the slope.

I could hear water running today under the ice and snow of Hope Creek.

■ *April 6th.* Plus twenty-two degrees. Overcast.

My alarm cord stirred me again about midnight. The wolverine was within fifty feet of the kitchen window, moving powerfully from side to side and stripping meat from the hide. It was quite dark with no moon shining, only the whiteness of the snow. When I caught him in the beam of the flashlight, he glared at me momentarily, but the light seemed too much for him and he loped with short rolling leaps into the dark.

This morning I spotted him coming across the lake. From his general direction I thought I knew where he was headed. As soon as he was out of sight, I ran for the cabin, grabbed my movie camera and snowshoes, and slogged through the timber to cut him off. Surely he would cross Hope Creek on the same track as before. A blurred movement through the scattering of spruce, and there he was, rocking along his trail. Not much of a picture at 200 yards, but much satisfaction in that I had guessed his move.

■ *April 11th.* Partly cloudy. Plus twenty-four degrees.

For the past several evenings I have tried to live-trap the wolverine. I built my trap out of the two halves of the fifty-gallon drum, hinged on one side so the weighted upper half would lift in a cocked position and slam shut when the bait trigger was pulled. I had visions of one mad wolverine. I figured he had more guts than brains, and his guts would get him into the jackpot. First get the meat, then get out of the trap, that would be his philosophy. But he never came, and finally I wrote him off as being on his delayed circuit calls beyond the mountains.

This morning as I came from woodsplitting detail, I saw a red fox near the live trap and the moose bait tied on a line. Why the fox didn't see me was hard to understand. I froze. Just like a red fox would do with a fat hen from the chicken yard, he snatched up the meat in his jaws and lit out for the brush.

He didn't figure on the line being tied on the other end, and when the slack ran out, the line whipped tight, the meat flew out of his mouth. He calmly turned around as much as to say, "Why, of course. You have to untie it first." In less than five seconds he was trotting triumphantly to the brush with the meat. I looked at the cord. It was cut as if with a knife. How about that for being smart as a fox?

Later I climbed the ladder to the cabin roof and rapped the stovepipe a few licks to knock down some soot and make the stove draw better. I happened to look down the lake. Something black was on the ice. I scrambled down the ladder for my binoculars, through which I saw a big black wolf with a white patch on his chest and another one, light-colored, lying down near the shore.

No doubt they saw me but couldn't figure out what they were looking at. They hunched on the ice quite a ways apart, then decided they had come close enough to this strangeness. Off they went toward Emerson Creek.

■ *April 16th.* A crust on the snow. Scattered clouds. Plus twenty-five degrees.

It has been more than three weeks now since Babe was last here.

This morning the beating of wings startled me. Spruce grouse were moving through, whirring from tree to tree. I saw the rooster puffed up like a balloon on the snow, tail fanned and wing tips dragging as he drifted over the crust. He ignored me completely. Skin patches were tufted above his eyes like bright red flowers. The feathers on his neck stood straight out. His fan tail flicked and winked almost as if it were rotating, and he made a noise that sounded like two pieces of fine sandpaper rubbing together.

As he came within two feet of me he stopped, shrugged his inflated body and flipped his tail in a gesture that seemed to say, "Step aside, Bud, and let a man past." And off he strutted over the snow. In the shadows of the spruce the females seemed absolutely bored with the entire performance.

The old rooster feels spring coming on strong. That's a good sign.

■ *April 17th.* Plus thirty-five degrees. The icicles dripping.

I saw the weasel for the first time in several weeks. I do believe he is starting to turn to his summer coat. It is getting cream-colored in places.

When I was up on the Cowgill benches looking for ptarmigan, Babe came. He was unloading on the ice when I reached the cabin. All kinds of supplies. Mary had started plants in her greenhouse. His boys were cutting house logs. Yes, those little spruce grouse roosters this time of the year will walk up and peck you on the shoe. Ptarmigan will do the same. And a man could tame a wolverine if he had lots of meat. Babe knew of one that had packed a trapper's snowshoes away and the trapper never did find them. Oh yes, he just might be back on Sunday with the one-eighty and bring the mission girls.

I had heard that before.

■ *April 19th.* Plus eighteen degrees. Clear and calm.

He did come back! Babe in the one-eighty, with passengers! Surely he had brought the mission girls. I counted three others besides Babe, a man and two women.

Babe had brought his wife, Mary, and a young school teacher and his wife. The mission girls couldn't get away today.

We had a nice visit. Mary toasted marshmallows in the fireplace for all hands. Babe suggested the young couple sing a song or two. Both had strong, clear voices and the songs were hymns, of course. There sat Babe basking in the warmth of the fire, his head bowed, his eyes closed as if asleep in the Hereafter. Surely he enjoyed the singing more than anyone.

The teacher left to take some pictures of my cabin, and no sooner had he left than he returned. He was noticeably excited. "A bird lit in my hand," he said.

I got out the can of meat scraps, and the teacher and his wife were like little children as they held out their hands and the birds came to them.

They sampled some of my blueberries from the cooler box. Better than fresh picked, they said.

Babe grinned at me as he climbed into the pilot's seat. "I'll bring the girls next trip," he said.

They all waved, and off they went over the ice.

■ *April 22nd.* Fog halfway down the mountains. Plus twenty degrees and calm.

I climbed up past the hump and picked a two-pound coffee can of big, firm, dull red cranberries. I dumped them into a pan to cook them in their own juice. I stirred the berries around a bit and picked out the sticks, moss, and leaves. A fistful of sugar was next, followed with a shot of corn syrup, a few wooden spoonfuls of Mrs. Butterworth's syrup, and a generous spill of honey. Soon the potion was bubbling away. I mashed the plump berries with the spatula. When the mixture cooled, I poured it off into empty bottles. Now those sourdoughs would have an elegant topping in the morning.

A strange object appeared halfway up the slope of Allen Mountain just under the rock outcrops. It changed shades. It was a bear. I ran for the big spotting scope. Sure enough, a big blonde bear and then another, chocolate color, and another, until there were three standing half as tall as the mother. Cubs, but not this year's.

They were digging for roots or ground squirrels and rattling an occasional boulder down into the timber. Now and then I could hear a growling followed by the cubs bawling their answers. I saw one cub start a rock going and stand there spraddle-legged following its progress as if contemplating the wonder he had wrought. If they made as much racket all the time, it would be no trouble locating this crew at work. The last I saw of them the old mother had lain down nearly on her back, and the little guys moved in for supper.

A bunch of sheep bedded down on the skyline high above them.

It is good to see bears on the mountain again—a mother and three fine-looking cubs. Good company for a man out here.

■ *April 23rd.* Calm and plus twenty-one degrees. Moon nearing the half.

I spent the day following a fresh wolf track to the upper end of the lake and beyond.

I saw a cow moose and calf leaving the country. Very interesting when I came to where the wolf track intersected with their trail. The cow had led her yearling down the running creek. I found where she had crossed over two ice bridges. This was definite evidence of the wisdom of the wild. She had succeeded, temporarily at least, in giving the wolf the slip by taking to the water.

Many ptarmigan in the willow flats, a regular convention. The roosters are full of cackle, with bright red splashes over their eyes, their heads and necks a glinting copper color. They are fast coming out of winter plumage.

Those cubs are wrestling and rolling like balls on the grassy slopes. Such carrying-on up there in the high country.

Several eagles sailed the thermal updrafts this evening. There is a wild freedom about their presence.

■ *April 24th.* Fifteen degrees.

The falls across the lake is trickling a very tiny stream.

A wedge of about fifty swans flew high and rained their music down on the land. They sound happy to be back.

Time to retire the snowshoes.

■ *April 30th.* Thirty-three degrees. A strong breeze down the lake.

I spotted the bear family again today. The cubs were playing "King of the

Hill" on a snowbank. One of the little guys put on quite a show, waltzing with a small cottonwood. He tried to climb a larger one with no apparent success. The old mother appears to be unconcerned about their antics, but the way she tips and tosses that muzzle into the air, you know she is on the alert all the time.

Ants on the ice—but in the glasses they were caribou, five head trailing across from the gravel bank toward Emerson Creek.

When they disappeared, I decided it was time for an Emerson Creek patrol. Off I went over the ice.

Bear tracks were mixed with the caribou tracks in the gravel. I moved on to the top of the rise and saw about thirty-five cows—but no calves yet.

Two caribou bulls on the flats, with new antlers more than a foot high.

A small trickle of water courses beneath the ice flakes on the mud banks. The clear song of a robin is heard now and then.

The days of snow and ice are numbered.

– *Breakup* –

■ *May 4th.* Feathers of blowing snow. Thirty-two degrees.

Back in late November I had cut my cache logs at the far side of Hope Creek, about forty of them, and I had peeled the frozen bark with a drawknife. These logs were four to six inches through at the butt. I had cut four other heavier logs about fifteen feet long and seven inches in diameter at the butt, and peeled them also. These would be my stilts to hold the cache aloft. The logs had been seasoning all this time.

It is my birthday today. I spent it chasing the bear family, and they obliged with what I hope will be some fine pictures.

This evening the robins are singing.

For my special supper, a thick ram steak fried in a salted skillet. Red in the middle with the juices running all over the plate. Blueberries for dessert.

This country makes a man younger than his birthdays.

■ *May 6th.* Thirty-five degrees. A light breeze down the lake.

I was up at four. I looked out, and there under the trees no more than thirty-five feet from the cabin door was the largest rabbit I have ever seen in my life, at least two feet tall. It was still snow white except for a dark trace in its ears. It had to be an arctic hare. Its ears worked like a pair of scissors and its nose twitched as if with an itch within it couldn't reach. Then it flowed into motion, traveling like a ghost off into the shadows.

■ *May 7th.* An inch of snow during the night. Clear, calm, and twenty degrees.

Tracks of Super-Rabbit outside my cabin door. Still a good tracking snow, so I decided to find out something about him. He was a busy rabbit. The snow was all packed down around some willow brush where he had fed. Then I came to the smooth, snow-covered creek ice, which must have been a speedway to him. He really got into high gear. I measured a good fourteen feet between the tracks of the hind feet. His hind foot track, where he sat down, measured a shade better than six inches in length and a strong two and a quarter inches in width. The arctic hare is no midget.

Today I would see about the postholes for my cache stilts. The ground was not nearly as frozen as I had thought, but many rocks made for hard digging. I packed water and dumped it into the holes. This helped some. I decided to let the water set in the frost to hasten the thawing.

I cut my heavy stilt poles to length. The cache will sit at least nine feet off ground level, which should put it better than five feet above the winter snows. I plan to angle the stilts in a bit and run the upper ends at least two feet up into the corners of the inside of the cache. This should make the cache itself solid on the stilts without side bracing.

To set the stilts at an angle and extend the upper ends into the cache corners, I would have to make a bend about two and a half feet from the upper end of each post. After a few unsuccessful experiments, I gave up and sawed off the post ends, and just hewed a flat place on which to anchor the little house to its platform.

Like the cabin and the fireplace, I can see the cache up on the poles.

■ *May 8th.* Snow showers. Thirty degrees.

A kettle of lima beans bubbled on the stove while I deepened my postholes. Babe came sliding in on the skis. Something very special this time, a fancy chocolate cake. Sister Florence had sent Babe's wife money to bake me a birthday cake.

I popped a pan of popcorn in some bacon grease, and soon we were munching away. No, he hadn't seen arctic hares around Lake Clark. He might bring the mission girls out to see my cabin one of these days, maybe while the ice was still good. After a slice of my birthday cake, he took off in a swirl of snow and disappeared over the volcanic mountains.

I read my mail and went back to my posthole project. The holes are now thirty-two inches deep.

I must sprinkle a fresh coat of gravel on my floor and the path out front. That threat of the mission girls arriving causes me no end of extra laundry, not to mention dusting and keeping things in reasonable order.

I can hear the sound of the small waterfall over on Falls Mountain this evening.

■ *May 9th*. The sun lighted the cabin logs at four-thirty this morning. Soon the sun will clear the mountains completely and there will be sunshine in the valley all day.

I watched a chickadee going in and out of a knothole in the big spruce near the clothesline. Instead of packing material in, she was packing it out, rotten wood from inside the tree. Should be a nest there soon. Today the frozen snow sparkles with the blaze of billions of diamonds. A very wide wedge of snow-white swans flew against the dark blue sky. Caribou bulls on the upper end of the lake. Many sheep on the mountains. Lambing time draws near.

■ *May 10th*. Twenty-six degrees. Hope Creek broke through the ice today and flowed on top down along the far side.

A pair of hoary redpolls. The little male looks as if he had a can of red paint spilled on his head and down his vest. Many small birds are here now. An eagle, circling low along the slope, let out a war cry. Does he do this to flush his prey out of hiding?

■ *May 11th*. Saw a sight today. As Babe would say, "Now wasn't that something?"

It was a beautiful spring morning. I decided to climb up through Low Pass and take a look at the Kigik River country. The snow crust kept breaking through but I finally made it over the pass to my favorite rocky knoll overlooking the big basin of the Kigik River. The sun was warm as I glassed the surroundings.

I picked up the trail of a lone caribou in the lenses and had just caught up with the cow when I saw her turning suspiciously. Something else caught my eye—a calf and a very small one. The cow was working toward me, and on her heels the wobbly legged calf. I hoped they would keep coming but the calf lay down. The cow browsed about and finally settled down beside it.

She had picked a good place to have her calf. There was very little chance of a wolf finding her here. Soon she was on her feet again. But at that moment I spotted a bear in the snow basin. His course would take him right to them.

The cow saw him and knew it was danger. She headed my way, stopping and nudging the calf to follow. The little one hurried as best it could, which was none too fast. The cow trotted and waited, trotted and waited.

Then the bear saw them and broke into a lumbering run. On they came, the calf doing its best with its legs going in all directions. I knew it wouldn't make it. They would pass me at 100 yards along the top edge of a high bench with an open rock slide face.

The bear was coming on fast. He would catch the calf near my stand. The end of the bench pitched steeply into deep snow and the cow ploughed into it. But it was too much for the calf. It bogged down in the snow, calling, *How! How!*

The cow stood in the snow at the foot of the bench, looking up. Still bawling, the calf struggled to the rocks. On came the bear along the top edge. If I had had the ought-six along, I would have changed his mind in a hurry.

Then a strange thing happened. The bear seemed unaware of the calf in front of him. His mind was on the cow and he took a shortcut across the slide, rattling rocks down in his haste to get to her. He passed less than forty feet below the calf. When he hit the snow on the dead run, he ploughed along on his muzzle and nearly upended. The cow leaped in panic down the canyon toward the upper lake, the bear helter-skelter on her heels. I was shaking with the excitement of the scene.

The little calf struggled across the steep, snow-covered slope. It lost its balance and collapsed in a heap. As I approached, it lay very still, head outstretched on the snow. I don't think it was a day old.

As much as I wanted to comfort the calf, I decided not to bother it. I would wait for the cow to return. Would she come back? Had the bear caught up to her?

Two hours passed and still the calf lay there in the snow. I would move it to a patch of dry grass, scent or no. I picked it up. The little doe was limp as a rag. I laid her on the dry mat of grass and she lay there very still. Suddenly she got to her feet and tottered toward the rock slide. This would never do. She started climbing faster and I cut her off. Then she turned and began to grunt and came right toward me. She thought I was her mom. I caught her and tied her four legs together with my bandanna. I left her resting easy in a sheltered warm place and followed the bear tracks to the head of the canyon. Those big claws were really digging in and I could see the long leaps the cow had taken in the snow. I waited and watched, but saw nothing.

Finally I went back to the little orphan. I could see the red bandanna before I saw her. They really blend in with their natural surroundings, I thought.

She was gone! The bandanna was still knotted. I picked up her trail and found her bedded down about 100 yards down the slope.

It was getting late and it was now snowing. I hated to leave her. What if the cow did not come back? Had the bear dragged her down? I decided to pack the little girl to my cabin, and return with her in the morning. If the cow did come back in the night, she would probably stay in the area for a spell.

What a tussle! She struggled and blatted, *How! How!* as I tied her legs together and pushed her rear end down into the front pocket of my ammunition bag. She was so small that only her neck and head stuck out, and I felt like a mother kangaroo with a young one peering out of the pouch. For a time she churned and twisted to get out, calling out, *How! How!* over and over again. I kept bucking the deep snow with the little noise-maker-squirming below my chest. Finally her struggles lessened and her *hows* became grunts. She began to work her mouth. The little tyke was getting hungry, and she rubbed her nose against my face.

The lake at last. Her eyes were closed and her head resting against my arm as we covered the last two miles to the cabin.

I turned her loose inside. She was pretty wobbly at first but soon she got around, nosing here and there. She fell over the potato box and finally lay down in front of the fireplace.

What to feed her? I had some non-fat powdered milk. I boiled and strained oatmeal, added a little sugar and some honey and a drop or two of vinegar. She was up rubbing against me before it was done. I took a clean white rag, saturated it with the mixture and put it to her mouth. She sucked my finger. I decided she was going to make it.

She curled up in the middle of the gravel floor and seemed happy as a new baby caribou could be under the circumstances. What should I name her? I thought I would call her Mae, as it was the month of May when she became my orphan.

Perhaps I should have walked away and left her on the mountain. If I had, I don't think I would have slept at all.

■ *May 12th.* Well, I didn't sleep anyway.

A baby caribou has a loud and penetrating voice. Its vocabulary consists of three words: . . . *how! ow!* and *uh!* She used them all through the night and, in addition, rattled everything that was loose in the cabin. I fed her at ten, at twelve, and at three. She even tried to climb into my bunk but finally settled for just curling up beside it.

When I opened the door this morning, she scrambled out and picked around here and there. Her neck is barely long enough to reach the ground without spreading those front legs. I measured her. Two feet tall, level with her back, legs sixteen inches, two and a half feet from nose to tail, and width an amazing four inches!

I was soon off to Low Pass with her. She didn't want to ride in the pouch so I turned her loose. She trotted along behind like a dog, those long legs tangling and untangling on the slippery rocks of the beach. I picked her up in my arms and walked the lake ice. When she began to struggle, I put her down again. She slowly tagged along, but before long her mouth sagged open. In a small snow patch she lay down and licked the ice from her tiny hooves in true caribou fashion.

Ride and walk, ride and walk. At the foot of Low Pass she curled up in the snow and closed her eyes. It would be a hard climb up the trench. I put her into the front pouch. As I climbed, she didn't make a sound, not even a move. Now and then I scooped up a handful of snow and she licked at it.

Through the saddle and finally to the scene of yesterday. Sure enough, caribou tracks backtracking the trail of yesterday right to where the little doe had collapsed. I should have left her as she lay. The cow had returned and had checked the surrounding bare spots. I glassed the slopes and the basin thoroughly, but not a caribou was in sight. The mother probably had headed for the Kigik. She hadn't found her calf so she had given up and left. There was only one thing for me to do—bring the little girl back to the cabin and hope for the best.

On the trip back, my passenger was quiet. Now and then she licked my hand and rubbed alongside my ear with her nose. She was not too lively when I unloaded her, probably tired from the long trip. I put her down in the warm sun and fed her. She lay quietly, nibbling weakly at some small brush. But she didn't call out as before. She just wasn't acting right. She lay stretched out instead of curled up as before. When I checked her again, she was warm but stiff and dead. How I wished I had left her on the mountainside!

■ *May 13th.* New snow on the high peaks. Thirty-two degrees.

I skinned the little caribou, fleshed and salted the hide, and puttered around the cabin wondering what the cow was doing.

Spring is coming on fast. The slopes are showing tinges of green. Some flowers are in bloom, and the cottonwoods are budding out. Mosquitoes are beginning to appear.

I set up the spotting scope for an inspection of Falls Mountain across the lake. New lambs, six of them with nine ewes. I studied them through the 60-power eyepiece and finally talked myself out of climbing up there among them to see them at close range. I had a cache to build.

I finished the postholes and set in the big stilts for the cache, along with a set of two braces for each post to get them all in place at the proper angle. I backfilled and tamped the gravel and rock around the butts with a pole stomper. Then I packed water and poured it around the bases. When it was all solidly in place, the braces were removed. I'm now ready to square off the tops of the big stilts.

Many flocks of geese, like hounds driving overhead. No real evidence of a caribou migration yet.

■ *May 14th.* The camp robbers were early for breakfast this morning.

A mighty roar from Crag Mountain startled me. I looked up in time to see tons of snow unloading from a high, narrow wash and spreading down the slope to blanket my cranberry patch. To be below when all that broke loose would be enough to frighten a man.

Time to saw my cache stilts to just the proper length and pack more gravel, sand, and rocks to heap around their bases. Mosquitoes were busy but no little gnats yet. They are the worst pests of all.

Lots of cabin chores today. A big wash was strung on the line, flopping and snapping in the breeze from down country. My sleeping bag was aired with all the scents of spring in the mountains.

■ *May 15th.* Hope Creek is running a good stream into the lake but it has not opened a channel in the lake ice yet.

Made some large deposits in the woodpile savings account today. Noticed some rosettes of rhubarb pushing through. Checked the thickness of ice at the waterhole. Thirty-two inches and solid. I formed a huge O.K. with spruce boughs in a place where Babe could easily see it and know the ice was still safe to land on. I hope he comes before it leaves a question mark in a man's mind. I would hate to have him land and sink out of sight. He probably wouldn't mind though. Says he's ready to go anytime at all.

■ *May 16th.* Twenty-four degrees. New ice on the open holes along the lakeshore.

Learned a valuable lesson today. I took a long tour down to the lower lake, three hours one way. After traveling over a low saddle of loose rock, I came upon a grass-covered valley and saw caribou, many cows and newborn calves. I had stumbled on the caribou maternity ward.

Those little ones fed every hour or less and they moved very little. I got so carried away at what was going on in the pasture, I forgot all about time. It was now late in the afternoon and I had at least three hours of travel ahead of me. On my way, I broke out into a stand of small spruce trees whose bark had been stripped last fall by caribou bulls rubbing the velvet from their antlers. I wish I had known they were there.

A strong wind was blowing when I reached the cabin. I got a fire going. It seemed sluggish so I rapped the stove pipe a few times and the fire came to life. Soon a strange odor came to me. I went outside and saw smoke pouring from the roof. I ran for the water bucket and sloshed it on the trouble spot.

That took care of the emergency, but not before the fire had burned through the polyethylene and the tar-paper. Let that be a lesson. Never rap on the stove pipe with the fire going. The draft had carried a chunk of hot soot up and dropped it in the dry moss. After this there will be fire inspection before I leave the diggings. And the moss will be kept damp. It would really shake a man up to return and find the cabin burned to the ground.

■ *May 17th.* Strange to wake up before three in the morning and feel that daylight is being wasted.

Today I repaired the roof. Found three damaged spots which I covered with new pieces of polyethylene and tar paper, making it better than before. The stovepipe was badly burned and rusted out, nearly the full length of one joint open along the seam. I got out the new sections of four-inch stored in Spike's cabin and installed them upside down to keep them free of creosote. I needed a spark arrestor, and the one-eighth-inch mesh screen that brother Jake had sent for sand screen would be just right. I made a tube of it four inches in diameter and eighteen inches long, and put the Chinese hat on top of it.

There is a narrow strip of open water next to shore due to the lake rising from the melting snows. How much longer will the lake be safe to land on? No big cracks in the ice yet.

This afternoon I prepared to build my cache. I packed all the peeled logs to a good, level spot on the beach. Here the chips would be easy to clean up. I put down a couple of planks I had ripped earlier, for a level foundation to build upon. Center to center each way, forty-seven inches and sixty-eight inches. I am anxious to see it up on the stilts.

■ *May 18th.* Who can go back to bed after the sun is up?

The camp robbers rattled the spruce buck-horns time and time again until I got breakfast going.

The first course of logs was notched and nailed to my foundation planks. I cut notches for four floor stringers and hewed the stringers to fit. I will add the floor when I take the whole structure apart for moving and assembly on top of the stilts.

I spotted a bear with three small cubs as I was glassing the mountains after lunch. With the spotting scope mounted nearby, I checked on the family at intervals while I worked. Those little fellows really love to play and mix it up in the midst of all their grubbing activities on the mountainside.

Eleven logs in place, plus the floor stringers, by late afternoon. A good start.

■ *May 19th.* There they were at six o'clock, high in the rough stuff above the grubbing grounds, the old sow in the lead with the three cubs trailing. I watched them until they went over the edge to the big sheep pasture and out of sight.

Another day to make chips. The logs fitted snugly into their custom-made notches.

Tonight finds thirty in place. The cache is now twenty-nine inches high.

Does the lake ice melt from the top down or the bottom up?

▪ *May 20th.* Wind bags in the sky. Those small oval clouds usually forecast high-velocity winds.

More cache-building today. Forty logs in place, three feet high to the square. The gable logs are put up and the ridge log is in place. Now for some roof poles, which are cut to length, ready and waiting.

Everything has a good, snug fit down here on the ground. I hope it goes together with no trouble when I climb the ladder with all the pieces. This is the first pre-fab cache at Twin Lakes.

The lake level is rising but the ice is still thirty-two inches thick. The border of open water around the lake is dimpled with rain this evening. A gentle spring shower is in progress.

▪ *May 21st.* Those wind bags yesterday told the story ahead of time. Wind blowing a gale this morning.

One year ago today Babe brought me here to Twin Lakes. We sat and talked on the gravel bar at the upper end of the lower lake. I had backpacked two loads that day up to Spike's cabin and had even picked up a sunburn from the sun on the snow. It was the first day of what I believe has been the most interesting year of my life.

Now it is another day to make chips and sawdust. The floor poles must be cut to length. It is blowing much too strongly for any work on the cache ladder.

I used the long ladder to bridge the moat of open water and get out on the ice. It is twenty-eight inches thick, a shrinking of four inches from yesterday. I doubt Babe will come until ice is out, unless he comes on floats and lands in the open water at the outlet of the connecting stream.

The wind carried rain with it in the afternoon. Not a day to work outside.

I went to the woodshed and ripped out planks for the door frame of the cache, and some one-and-a-half-inch planks for the twenty-by-twenty-three-and-a-half-inch door. I cut two sets of hinges out of stump wood.

I am thinking the lake will rise considerably from this storm, as no doubt it is raining hard in the high mountains and the water will come pouring down the slopes. The more rain and wind the better now, because it will speed the breakup of the lake ice.

▪ *May 22nd.* Forty degrees and still sprinkling. The wind blew itself out last night.

The lake ice is now twenty-four inches thick and still plenty solid. Under a bright sun the ice has changed from green to a snow-white. The lake is steadily rising and the open water around its edges is widening. If I travel the ice today, I might have trouble getting off.

I was ready to take my little log house apart and put it back together again on top of its nine-foot stilts.

Three sharp calls from a camp robber, meaning danger in the area. Twice more I heard the alarm signal, then I saw a hawk flashing through the spruces.

I used my meatpole ladder for a scaffold. Soon number-one log was resting atop the stilts, but it was past six o'clock and I decided to call it a day. Tomorrow evening should see the cache all assembled in its new location.

While I was eating supper, a pair of red-breasted mergansers cruised down the stretch of open water, upending out of sight and feeding under the ice. When they bobbed to the surface, they looked dry as corks.

The camp robbers came with no battle scars. The hawk had something else for dinner.

Hope Creek is now back in its regular channel and running under ice nearly three feet thick in places.

▪ *May 23rd.* Clear, calm, and twenty-five degrees.

Today would be my high-rise construction day. I made certain I had a good bearing surface on the ends of the posts. I mixed a batch of glue and sawdust to insure a real good fit at each corner. Two sixty-penny spikes also were driven into each of these important areas.

I still was not satisfied. I had salvaged some one-inch-square tubing from a wrecked Tripacer aircraft at the upper end of the lake. It would come in handy now. I augered a seven-eighths-inch hole through each log on the four corners and on down into the top of each post. Then I drove a length of tubing into each of these holes with the heavy axe. In the process, I knocked the logs three-quarters of an inch off of square. A line from one front corner to the opposite rear corner pulled it square again.

The logs fitted perfectly. Forty-penny spikes went into the heavy ends and sixteen-pennies into the small ends. Eaves logs, gables, ridge log—a smooth operation. The fitting time spent on the beach really paid off. When noon arrived, I was just finishing up with the roof poles. I never expected the structure to go up so quickly.

Next the door. The logs forming the top and bottom of the opening were already partly sawed through, so all that remained was to cut the logs in between. And I had the opening for the door.

The roof covering was a course of tar paper, a sheet of polyethylene, a layer of moss, and poles to hold the moss down, same as for the cabin.

■ *May 24th.* A ram stew on the fire first thing. Soon the ram will be all cleaned up. It was a lot of fine eating.

The lake ice is now twenty inches thick and still safe to travel. The problem is getting off it once you are on. The water temperature in the shallows is thirty-eight degrees.

■ *May 25th.* A skim of ice on the open water. With the water level up like it is, the ice must be free to shift. Surely it has cracked all the way across in places, but it shows no sign of shifting at all.

I should be able to finish the cache today. I turned out a long, curved fancy door handle with a latch to put on the end of it. I am really proud of that piece of work. That door and handle look happily married. I chinked with a little oakum and lots of moss. For all practical purposes, my miniature cabin on stilts was complete.

How one thing leads to another! My fifteen-foot meatpole ladder is too big for the cache. Tomorrow I will make an eleven-footer.

A few jobs to do in the late afternoon—repair my shoes, which are too good to throw away and not good enough to keep, plus tools to sharpen and saws to file.

■ *May 26th.* The mountain slopes are misted with green. The leaves are unfurling unbelievably fast. Cottonwood buds are opening.

My ladder project had priority today. I had a perfect pole that was well seasoned. I ripped it down the center and put my ladder together with the flat sides in. The steps were short logs with flat sides up and level, making a ladder a man could walk up instead of climb. I put it all together with nails and glue.

I sat on the beach munching on a cold sourdough-hotcake sandwich, and who should come along the open-water highway but a beaver, no more than forty feet away. He swam back and forth, staring at me. Then he disappeared as if he were jealous of a character who could pile up more chips than he did.

A butter-flecked sunset, with the temperature at fifty-seven degrees. I had all I could do to get out on the lake ice this evening, and was surprised to find it only twelve inches thick. Babe had said, "As long as it is safe for landing, leave the big wood block out that marks the waterhole. I can see it good from the air."

The block is no longer on the ice.

I suppose the wood block would be the same as the oil drum on the ice. "When the ice is safe," Babe said, "put the oil drum on the ice." I did. Ten weeks later he came in and asked me, "Why the oil drum on the ice?" He has a good memory, but it isn't very long.

■ *May 27th.* Thirty-two degrees. Overcast and a strong wind up the take.

Hope Creek is pouring a big volume of water from its mouth. This turmoil plus the wave action from around the point are rapidly eating away the ice. I could see the pool of open water growing before my eyes.

It began to snow big flakes, four inches on the ground before it stopped. Then a big blue spot turned on in the cloud cover, and the sun broke through. A beautiful sight. I hurried to Spike's cabin and rushed the canoe out of retirement. Late last fall I had been happy to put it away, but now I was happy to slide over the water again, in the wide channel between the shore and the edge of the rotting ice. I just had to take some pictures of my cabin and the new addition from offshore.

▪ *May 28th*. Forty degrees. The mountains are white from the snow of yesterday.

An odds-and-ends day. I made a screen for my kitchen window. Now I can open the window at night and not be annoyed by the singing of mosquitoes. I washed the caribou calfskin in soap and water. It is a pretty little hide about as big as a bandanna. Next I wrapped a twelve-inch band of gas tin around each leg of the cache at a point eight inches from the top. I would like to see that juvenile delinquent of a squirrel, or any other climbers, bypass that barrier.

I grubbed out a path to the cache and packed it with beach gravel. Cleaned up some building chips and drove in a water gauge stake for measuring the lake level.

Much more open water now. Piles of ice pushed up a ridge across the lake as it moved down from the upper end.

▪ *May 29th*. A day of organization.

Sorting, transferring, storing gear away in the cache, winter clothes to box up. My big white sheepskin and the curled horns, the extra grub. There was room to spare when I finished packing everything up high. Not room enough for a large moose, but space left for another ram or a caribou. It is all stowed now and with the ladder down, not even a mouse can get in—that is, if I didn't pack one up there.

I found out why I didn't see too much of the squirrel this past winter. I discovered many piles of spruce-cone flakes where he had eaten under the snow. Not many spruce trees have hollows in them, but I have seen tunnels into their root systems. I'm sure squirrels do this.

Come to think about it, I have seen mine snipping off green cones, letting them fall every which way. He must collect them later and store them in his tunnels. Then when snow covers the land, he keeps out of sight beneath it, hauls a cone out of storage and dines in snowlight.

Used up the last of my sheep meat today. It has been more than eight months since I packboarded that big ram down the mountain in two loads.

■ _June 6th._ The great ice chunks are moving past at the rate of fifty feet a minute. The chime-like tinkle of the crumbling ice was a welcome sound.

Wind is building up and whitecaps toss on the dark green water. After six and a half months of ice, the lake is nearly free and the mountain peaks can look at themselves in the mirror again.

– *Cloud Country* –

■ *July 2nd.* Still, with mist rising from the slopes of the mountains. Forty-five degrees.

I would go up high today. After yesterday, which was the day of the lost axe, I had to take a little trip. Much wasted time and I almost suffered a touch of cabin fever. It all started when I decided to trim out a dead spruce and buck it into lengths that I could pack to the woodshed.

The axe! It was gone from its rack in front of the cabin! What had I done with it?

I looked all over the place. No axe. After all the miles we had traveled together building everything, I hated the thought of losing it. A man could no more afford to lose his axe out here than he could his wallet full of folding money in a strange city.

I tried to retrace my steps over the last several days. I went to where I had limbed out the last tree. Not there. I looked in the woodshed and turned the woodpile upside down. Not there either. Another search of the cabin. In an area only twelve feet by sixteen feet, it didn't seem as though I could miss it. Under the mattress pad, on the floor under the bunk, in the corners, behind the closet, behind the book rack.

Suddenly the trail got warmer. The bunk post next to the clothes closet stirred my memory. There was the axe, behind the post and above the ground so I couldn't see it from below. Why had I ever put it there in the first place?

I was so happy to feel its welcome heft once more. I ran my palms over its workworn handle, scoured the tree sap from it, filed its blades, honed them razor keen, and set it into a gas-can tin of water to swell the handle tight into the head.

It was a valuable lesson. This morning the double-bitted chip-maker is back in its rack. A place for everything, everything in its place. Whoever said that knew what he was talking about.

Where would I head today to celebrate finding the axe? Up the Hope Creek cut and into the high basin at the foot of the glaciers? That is always an adventure. One way in, and you can't see out except at the lower end. It makes me think of the mountain hideout of the "Hole-in-the-Wall" gang. You go up across the rock slides where the little pikas squeak and leave their piles of grasses and wild pea vines to cure in the sun. Then that long look down at Hope Creek, its blue water a-sparkle, showing white here and there in its dash from the snow over the boulders.

Or how about the back slope of Crag Mountain and a visit to the hoary marmot colony? They are always interesting to watch, and to listen to their loud whistles. They're wary, always on the alert, as big as a fat Iowa woodchuck, with fur a beautiful silver white underneath and black tips on the hairs.

Or maybe across the lake and over the top of Falls Mountain? The lookout that covers the high valley of the many waterfalls—that would be a place to visit today, like going to a great outdoor theater with me the only human in the audience and the show continuous.

I would take the binoculars and spotting scope and leave the camera gear at home. My eyes paused at the rifle on the wall but I decided against it, too. I was headed for the country of big distances because I was in a spectator mood and did not want to be overloaded. It was the kind of day to go up high. It was very buggy at lake level though, and I would need headnet and gloves until I got above the insect pests.

Across the calm lake I paddled, through thousands of flying insects on the water. None were flying that I could see, and I wondered why they had to make forced landings? Many circles from rising fish. A fly fisherman would be kept

▲ *The Cowgill's bench shows off its autumn wardrobe.*

▲ *Dick found these white boulders, perfectly mated, at Glacier Creek. Weighing about 40 pounds each, they set off the lakeshore entrance of his gravel path, one on either side of it. He christened them "Grizzly Eggs." Notice the weathered caribou rack. No need to mow the lawn.*

▶ *(Clockwise top two rows). The bear paused during his blueberry feast to test the wind. Highbush cranberries for pancake syrup. One shot opened and closed the hunting season on a full curl ram. The potatoes broke no size records, but they were smooth-skinned. Fresh-picked blueberries to the brim.*

▲ *Blueberry foraging. Notice the connecting stream (upper left) that exits into the lower lake. The puddle-still lake reflects all images.*

▲ *(Clockwise from top left). A huge-racked caribou swims to evade an enemy. Green onions promise flavoring. A porcupine bristles his quills. The burbot looks like an eel mixed up with a codfish. It's ugly, but it has firm white flesh.*

▲ *Cabin windows glowing with lamplight beneath ice-glistening slopes. There is a hint of the aurora in the frosty stillness.*

▲▲ *Moonlit cabin under a snow mantling. Snowshoes ready to go.*

▲ *Fire's cheery flame glows within the facade of varicolored stones, which were collected from up and down both sides of the lakes. The cast of the wolf track above the orange stone in the arch measures 7" x 5".*

▲ *Hiking through a world that appeared to grow snow feathers. Soundless and motionless.*

▲▲ *Dick's pantry displaying his crafted accessories. Everything shipshape.*

▲ *Ready for company with double bunks mattressed with foam rubber pads. A handy cabinet. Beach gravel floor.*

▲ ▲ *Stove corner emanates order. Pots and skillets hanging from spruce pegs. A utility table. Everything has its place.*

▲ *Big window with a desk before it. A large storage shelf. Dick's sister had sent the curtains. Dick provided the rustic curtain rod and the driftwood sculpture.*

▼ *Best dressed man in the frost.*

▼ ▼ *A jumble of ice from the aftermath of breakup.*

▲ *Most of the lake white with ice. Allen's Mountain and Spike's Peak admire themselves in the lead of open water.*

▲ *Looking down from Cowgill's bench on Dick's complex. The spruces screen the lake.*

Beyond loom the snow-crowned peaks.

► *Dick had assembled this cache on the beach first. Then he took it apart and erected it piece by piece on the platform atop the stilts— an experiment with prefabrication. Notice his scaffold and ladder. Quite an aerial feat.*

▲ *Babe came on schedule. It was time to leave for the winter. Everything stored. One last look until spring.*

busy, but no fish for me today. They are always here and I could take them when I needed them.

As I rounded a brushy point there was a cow moose at the foot of a gravel bank. For a few minutes she stood and watched me, ears funneled. I sat motionless, my paddle blade dripping silver. She was the second cow I had seen without a calf. She scrambled awkwardly up the loose stones into the buckbrush, and headed in the direction of the big cottonwood park. Homely, ungainly, none of the majesty of the bull at all.

I beached the canoe high on the gravel, turned it bottomside-up, and tied it fast to a willow clump. Squadrons of gnats and mosquitoes were waiting to pounce on me, whining and biting. Bandanna knotted around my throat, headnet, cotton gloves, ammunition bag, and walking stick, I set out along the stony creek bottom.

Up ahead there was something brown and out of place. No rocks that size in the area. Through the binoculars I made out a high rack. What was a bull caribou doing down here where not a breath of air was stirring? I kept some brush clumps between us as I stalked closer. At less than 100 yards away I ran out of cover, so I just stayed put and watched him.

Insects were whirling around me like sawdust blown from a power saw. They were crawling over each other on my shirt and piling up on my gloves. The bull also was having a battle with the tiny fiends, stomping and shaking, twisting and turning and shivering his hide, lying down and getting back up again. He was rubbing his antler tips with his hind foot, flicking his ears, shaking his antlers violently—no rest at all.

Why doesn't he climb to a breeze or take a swim? Anything but stand and fight something he can't hope to kill or scare away. Well, if he didn't have better sense, maybe I could force his hand. With a yell and a waving of arms, I spooked him. He struck an almost dumbfounded pose for an instant and urinated. Then he threw his antlers back and off he clattered over the stones, eyes bulging, nostrils flaring, tail upright, and flashing white.

Away we go! Good luck to you, old boy.

I left the creek bed and climbed up through the spruce timber, over pillowy hummocks of sphagnum moss. A headnet is not to my liking while traveling, but a must today with the bugs as thick as they were. I stopped to examine a worn game trail that crossed my route. There has been very little traffic along it recently.

Out of the spruce, I climbed steeply through the cottonwoods and the highbush cranberry and the hellebore to the foot of the big rockface. I picked my way up and across it, keeping my body hugged against the granite and digging fingers into the handholds of the crevices.

One bad step and I would keep right on going down the mountain, but risk now and then is good for a man. Makes him come alive and tunes his body to a greater efficiency. Finally up and over the rock to the low bushes where fat blueberries were forming on the leafy twigs. Off to the left was the thin stream of the waterfall spilling over the black rim in a long drop to the circular pool below.

The steady ascent along the slope of the canyon, higher and higher. The chittering alarm of ground squirrels as they flicked away and did quick about-faces to peer from out the rocks.

Very few bugs now. It was a relief to shed the headnet and the gloves. Here were the first forget-me-nots of the season, some petaled as blue as the sky and golden centered, and some with pink flowers mixed into the bouquet. I stopped now and then to scoop a palmful of frosty water to my lips. There's no water in the world like that born in the high country.

Sheep droppings began to appear. Up, up, up to the big pasture that is such a pleasure to travel, with its slopes on either side rich with flowers. Orange, yellow, pink, blue, and white, dabs and smears of color like bright paints against the palettes of grass and moss. A cool breeze was stirring down from across distant glaciers. The gates of heaven are near.

Two ewes were skylined on the rimrock as I headed for my lookout knob in the upper pasture on Allen Mountain. Through the lenses I could see the beige coloration on their backs and flanks, the coal-black eyes peering out of their white faces as they studied the stranger on their mountain. They were shedding their heavy coats of winter.

Rags of fog now. The wisps blown on a damp wind from out of the snowfields, curling, spreading, disappearing. Finally, there it was, my observatory among the black boulders; two hours from the lowlands. No wonder the eagle soars the high places. Far below was the valley of Emerson Creek, with its many waterfalls in feeder streams that tumbled their courses from the snow saddle in the mists. Peaks all around me, some granite-ribbed and snow-blotched, some stabbing up starkly on either side of the glacier that curved between them like a great white, blue-rutted highway. Others were off in the direction of the lower lake, huge mounds of marble cake streaked in green shadows, all with a regal bearing that awed a man in their presence.

I unloaded my gear from the pouches of the ammunition bag, set up the scope on the tripod, and settled into the best seat in the house.

A pair of pipits were the first performers. They inspected the rocks that jutted out of the grasses behind, bobbing their tails constantly in the wind and flying short distances now and then to flash their white tail-feathers.

I trained the scope on what looked like a small mining operation in the slope across the valley. Bear diggings. Maybe all that energy pays off if the bear breaks into the bedroom. I could picture him busting into the main chamber of the den, ground squirrels going in all directions, and that shaggy intruder swatting with both forefeet, trying to scoop one up in his jaws.

Not too far away I spotted a mother brown bear with three cubs. It was probably the same family I had seen at different times during the spring. The cubs had grown and were lighter in color on their backs. The old sow was almost blonde, with her lower legs a dark brown. She was rounded out like a cask. Must be lots of vitamins along those slopes.

The bears were working slowly up country through the green alpine meadows. When they reached the creek, the old girl splashed out into a pool below a waterfall and appeared to take a bath while the cubs went at it in a free-for-all on the bank. All three were never in the hassle at the same time. The third one always stood aside, anxious to take on the winner.

I watched the ravens rising and floating and falling in and out of the mist above the crags that reared from the great snowfield. Their whoops and guttural yelps sounded as though they were coming over an amplifier in the vast stillness. They have a lot to talk about.

In the field of the big lens I picked up a set of bleached caribou antlers along the creek bottom. They were hitched together with a section of skull, and could not have been shed. I saw no other signs of bones about, so the bull had not just died there. Some hunter probably decided the antlers were too heavy to pack back to camp. I must examine them up close sometime. I might pack them back to the cabin and put them into my pile of antler finds.

Where were the caribou? Not one could I pick up at first. Then I saw a band of bulls on a high slope, some lying down chewing their cuds, others swaying their antlers, pulling at willow branches and dropping their heads now and then to graze along the ground. They looked in prime shape, white-bellied, white-bibbed, a mahogany chocolate sheen along the flanks and back. Some showed gray on their necks. These would wear those handsome white capes in late August and September.

I tried to examine one bull in particular through the 60-power eyepiece. His antlers were massive. On each side a branch curved out in back where none of the other racks did. He was double-shoveled. Those horizontal brow-palms seemed to match perfectly. Over and over again I tried to count his points, but he would move and I would lose my place and have to begin again. Forty-two to forty-five, I figured. They were magnificent to view, those heavy-beamed boughs of bone against the green of the slope. A trophy hunter would leave his wife for a head like that one.

There were many bands of sheep, ewes, and lambs scattered here and there. On a high pasture like an oasis in a desert of rocks, I spotted six big rams on Black Mountain. Two had better than a full curl. They were in their chosen isolation, wild mountain dandies living high off the grass away from the women and the kids.

Boulders of every size and shape showed in the rock slides. Some were splotched with orange lichens, some covered with growths that resembled dried flakes of leather. Others appeared as though smeared in places with brush swipes of red lead. Still others were just clean, many-sided chunks of granite. I had picked my way across those jumbles many times, always with the thought of stepping on the wrong rock, the key rock in the pile, and starting the whole slope into motion. Or slipping and jamming my foot down hard into a tapered space and not being able to pull it out again. Either way a man would have to settle with the Lord right there on the mountain.

Close at hand the mosses and grasses were full of tiny flowers. It is another world of beauty. The more I see as I sit here among the rocks, the more I wonder about what I am not seeing. Mine is only surface vision and poor at that, even with the powerful eye on the tripod and two others looped about my neck.

A flickering movement off to my left. The stones seemed to move, and turned into a mother ptarmigan and her brood, the young not fully grown but brown as their mother in her plumage of summer. They were feeding, huddled like chickens as they worked along the slope.

I checked on the bear family again. They were having lunch. The old sow was sprawled half on her back with the cubs gathered around her. They didn't take very long. Then they all bedded down for a nap, the cubs a study in sleeping positions—on their backs, legs in the air, on their sides as if flung there limp and lifeless. The old mother stretched out on her belly, head on her forepaws, claws agleam, seemingly dead to the world, but I knew only too well how fast she could come alive if the wind brought the man scent to her.

Clouds piled on the tops of some far peaks. A man could lose himself up there. I munched on my biscuit sandwiches, my eye following the flight of an eagle below. His white head and tail caught the sun as he searched beneath him. Sailing and circling, the wind currents lifting, gently buffeting him as he soared.

Everywhere I looked was fascination. Those great masses of broken rock that the mountain sheep bounced over as lightly as if on level ground. Chunks of the peaks falling away over the years had made these treacherous accumulations, like enormous tailing piles of giant prospectors.

Gleaming snowfields showed not a sign of a track. They would be blinding to walk across in the bright sun. And all those beautiful waterfalls, some dropping from the high buttresses like thin streams of molten silver and seeming to vanish in midair. Others along the creek below spilled in wide, bright aprons between banks as green as new leaves.

It was time to leave, so I picked up my walking stick. I had taken a long look into the heart of the high places and felt like a man inspired by a sermon that came to me firsthand, that came out of the sky and the many moods of the mountains.

When a man climbs high it always seems an amazement, as he starts down, to realize the distance he has covered. Going down is no easier than going up. It is more treacherous and you must be careful of your momentum. You feel the play of different muscles along your thighs and your shin bones as you jolt your way down the mountain.

I crossed the big pasture and took several sips of water from the trickles that made music over the stones—like a wine-taster not being able to decide which vintage was best. Down through the canyon with the rock-strewn slopes on either side and finally, just above where the canyon walls ran together, the triangular eye of turquoise that was the lake peered up at me.

A brief stop at the Eagle's Back, a dizzy jut of granite on the mid-slope of Falls Mountain. Climbing out on it, I stood feeling suspended over the entire upper lake that gleamed beneath in robin's egg blue. On the far side was the warm glow of logs that is home—the place I wanted to leave in the morning and the place I wanted to return to at the close of the day.

I thought I would just sit for a spell and glass the timbered bottom and the edges of the big cottonwood park for a glimpse of my giant bull. I might be lucky enough to catch him in the open. At one point I thought I saw a movement, a form that slowly changed shade, but a prolonged watch of the area revealed nothing more. I would check it out closer on the way down. I was happy that the temperature had dropped and the bugs were not as active as before. I was unhappy, though, that I couldn't find my walking stick when I started on down.

I broke out into the willows that grew around the edges of the cotton-woods. There were no fresh moose droppings or tracks. But then I came to a clump of cow parsnips freshly cropped and the grasses mashed around them.

Funny, I thought, I have never known a moose to eat this plant. I looked about. The leaves of the cottonwoods quivered against the sky. Suddenly the brush to my right rustled and crashed. I spun, expecting to see the bull getting up out of his bunk—and every hair on my head stabbed electricity into my skull.

A huge brown bear was coming head on, bounding through the willow clumps not fifty feet away! His head looked as broad as a bulldozer blade. I threw up my arms and yelled. That was all I could think to do.

On he came, and I thought, "At last you've done it, nothing can save you now." I was stumbling as I retreated in terror, shouting.

I tripped and fell on my back. Instinctively I started kicking at the great broad head as it burst through the willow leaves. And then as he loomed over me, a strange thing happened. The air whooshed out of him as he switched ends. Off he went up the slope, bunching his huge bulk, climbing hard, and showering stones. Not once did he look back.

I was shouting, encouraging him in his flight. What seconds before had seemed so terrifying was now almost comical. What had saved my skin?

He must have scented me at the last moment. Until then I do believe he had me pegged as another animal and meat on the table. I couldn't stop shaking. The rest of the way down the mountain I lived those seconds over and over again. I was convinced that the ought-six would be standard equipment from this day on.

As I pushed out in the canoe, it started to rain. On the surface film of the lake were little bubbles from the size of buckshot to grains of sand, each with a transparent silver crescent within it. Did the rain trap tiny pockets of air as it pelted into the surface?

The rain had eased to a dimpling on the lake when I beached the canoe on my landing. I looked down toward the lower end. A silver line on the surface telegraphed a breeze.

I lay awake for a long time. My mind kept returning to the bear.

– *The Red Runt* –

This is the red runt's country. I am the invader. Hardly a day passes that he does not remind me of that with his chatter, his mischief, and at times his downright vandalism. He makes his move and I make a counter move to block him the next time. In a way he is like a neighbor you would like to approach in an effort to settle your differences, but you find every attempt met with resentment and further misunderstanding until you finally give up the idea and make believe he isn't there.

I remember how he seemed to enjoy trailing the toilet paper among the spruce branches. That called for a tin-can cover to prevent further mischief.

Instead of helping himself to some of the blueberries on the cupboard shelf outside the cabin door, he does not seem to be satisfied until he has knocked the container to the ground and scattered berries in all directions.

Many times he has interrupted the rising of my sourdough biscuits when I placed them outside the cabin in the sunshine. I have rushed out the door on the heels of a clattering, to find my solar oven tipped over and my biscuits sprinkled with dry spruce needles. That little scamp leaps to a tree, scrambles up the trunk, and peers down pop-eyed at the mess.

When the magpies stole his food with their clever teamwork maneuvers, and he raced after the robbers that skimmed over the snow just beyond his grasp, I almost wished he could manage a mouthful of tail feathers.

He was the first one to raid the poncho-covered sheep meat when I had it hanging high in the meat tree. He tunneled right into good eating.

After the cache was completed, I prided myself for a long time on how animal-proof it was. Then the little aerialist launched himself to the roof one day while I was at the lower end of the lake. He discovered a small space near the ridge pole and chewed out an opening large enough to let him in.

My first clue to this breaking and entering was some white goose feathers curling to the spruce boughs nearby. I climbed to the cache. When I opened the door, there before me on top of my winter sleeping bag was a goosefeather nest. He had cut through the drawstring with his sharp teeth and ripped into the bag's innards. The result looked as though there had been an explosion through one side of the roll. He must have had feathers all over his whiskers.

One day while feeding my birds some meat scraps, I heard his scratchy approach down the bark of the big spruce. He was watching and seemed to be very interested. I held a scrap out to him. He moved toward it in jerks. How did he show his gratitude? He bit my finger hard into the nail bed and drew blood!

Why do I put up with the little scamp?

When I should have gloated over the weasel scaring him from his winter quarters in the woodshed, I found myself concerned about him.

His chewing shredded both my suspender straps so that they were hitched to the rain pants by threads. He gnawed the corner off my Styrofoam chest, leaving many popcorn-size chunks all over the ground. He bit through the clothesline before the wash on it had dried.

He has caused me no end of mending, many delays in my plans, and at times severe strain on my self-control. But in spite of all these things, in spite of his temper tantrum personality and his efforts to chase me out of the country, I continue to turn the other cheek. He was here first. I respect him as a resourceful member of the community, always making himself heard, full of mischief, forever curious—but always one to admire. He holds his own in all seasons with the best of them.

– *The Chilikadrotna* –

■ *August 25th.* Clear, calm, and twenty-eight degrees.

White frost on the brush and on the gravel of the beach. The lake like a huge puddle, grinning with the reflections of the fall colors well along on the mountains. Today was meant for canoe travel. I would go to the lower end of the lower lake where the Chilikadrotna River begins its long, swift journey to merge with the Mulchatna and the Nushagak, to pour their combined cargoes into Bristol Bay. It would be a paddle of eight and a half miles one way.

It was a joy to travel the flat lake. I dug the paddle deep and the canoe slid along easily, furrowing ripples to either side. The blade lifted with a crisp whisper, and a few silver drops twinkled as they dripped from it.

Near the lower end of the upper lake I spotted a fine caribou bull through the binoculars. He was heavy-racked and double-shoveled, with a snow-white cape and a streak of white running the length of his dark flank. He wore white oxfords, a real dandy. He was a long way from me but curious just the same. He trotted back and forth along the beach. Then a rearing whirl, antlers laid back, and off he went in that effortless floating trot so characteristic of the caribou.

The current caught me and I was swept into the throat of the connecting stream. On either side the banks flashed by. Just a dip of the paddle now and then to keep on course, and I shot out over the gravel bar onto the curling apron of the lower lake.

There was the caribou again, below the mouth of Bonanza Creek. I angled toward him. Off he trotted down the beach, up the bank and into the timber. He soon appeared about a half mile down and close to the beach. He was acting strangely. When I saw him wade into the lake, it dawned on me that he wanted to go to the other side.

Surely enough, he struck out for the far shore, just loafing along. I poured some power into the paddle. At about 300 yards he turned in the water to see me coming on strong. The race was on. He would show me how fast a bull caribou can swim.

The lake at this point was about three-quarters of a mile wide. I was gaining slowly, but I was beginning to doubt I could get ahead of him before he hit the beach. At not much more than 200 yards from shore, I turned him. This gave me a chance to ready my cameras and take some shots. I pulled in along his left side, trying to angle him in to the beach, but he wouldn't budge off course. I didn't want to get too close in case he turned on me. He could overturn the canoe with no trouble, and I would be in a jackpot then.

In some shallow water off a point, he hit bottom, lunged ahead in a shower, and made deep water again. I followed right after him. He was tiring and I could easily keep up with him now. He was breathing hard, snorting, and I was afraid he might drown. I pulled in front and turned him toward the beach, then dropped back to watch. Surely he would stand and rest when he struck the shallows.

Nothing doing. As soon as he had footing, he made the water fly. Up and on the beach and off through the brush as if he was not tired at all. Maybe he figured he couldn't get rid of me on land so he had done what he would have done with a wolf in pursuit—take to the lake. Swim and lose the enemy.

Ahead of me a loon was riding low in the water, a study in streamlining, diving, and bobbing up again an unbelievable distance from where he had disappeared. His laugh floated to me. "I'm over here!" he seemed to say. "Who are you in the canoe?"

In one of the bays I could see the bottom at least twenty feet down, and schools of trout. Not big trout, mostly char and lake trout about a foot long. Now and then a few bigger fish appeared, eighteen to twenty inches long, lying still on the bottom as I slid over them. Then in the area where the river began, hundreds of trout were clustered.

I headed for the beach before the current gripped me. I would have my hands full if I got caught in that funnel. Huge boulders reared out of white water, and I could hear the sound of its seething as it rushed out of the country.

I beached the canoe, strung up the fly rod, and picked my way along the bank. I tied on a small black fly, tested the knot, and stripped out some line. In the first two places I tried, the water was just too swift. The fly shot the line out straight in the blinking of an eye and dragged and bounced on the flow. A man couldn't wade out into that torrent; he'd get swept right off his feet.

Near a large boulder that jutted out into the river, the current slowed on the downstream side and made curlicues on the surface past overhanging willow brush. I cast just to the edge of the fast water and let the fly swing in an arc.

The grayling were there. They slashed viciously. A flick of the wrist and the rod tip quivered into a bow. The current exaggerated the fish's power, but it was graceful. It arced, high dorsal spread like a fan, and knifed back into the river again. Several times the line sawed back and forth as the grayling cut erratically to rid itself of the tiny fly. Finally exhausted, it slid into the fireweed that grew in the gravel.

It was a beautiful fish at least eighteen inches long, gill covers and tail a gleaming green and turquoise, body cylindrical with salmon-colored stripes on the fins. I released it. I caught several more, smaller that the first, then forced myself to keep the fly away from the feeding fish that swarmed beneath the willow branches.

I followed down along the bank until I came to a cabin. It belonged to a trapper named Frank Bell. The logs of the cabin walls were upended instead of laid parallel to the ground. It had been deserted for several years now. I creaked open the door.

"Hellooooooo, Frank," I called, almost expecting an answer from the gloomy emptiness. Some animals had raised havoc inside. There was a caribou robe on a sagging cot, some large traps hanging from pegs, and snares dangling from the walls. In a large iron pot were many dead mice. Once inside they had been unable to get back out.

Outside was a prominent meat pole high on the riverbank. Gas-can tins were wrapped around the uprights so animals could not climb to the crossbar.

I sat down with my back against a stump, my jaws working on a sourdough-pancake sandwich of peanut butter and honey, and listened to the wild rushing noises the river made over the great boulders. The Chilikadrotna? What did its name mean? Did Frank Bell know? I thought about him. I tried to imagine him coming out of his cabin, and suddenly felt a strange kinship with the man.

He and his Indian friend had told me stories back at Port Alsworth, and now the stories held more meaning. I could almost see the ghostly figures of the Indian packers with their 100-pound loads—no packboards, just ropes—backs bent as they trekked through the brush of the riverbank. They built rafts using only axes and no nails. They chopped upside-down notches in the logs, the cuts narrow at the top and flaring out at the bottom. Then they hewed out two three-sided poles, lined up the logs, and drove the poles into the triangle-shaped notches. Ends of the poles were split and wedges driven in to keep the poles snug in the logs. A finished raft was only four feet wide, yet they crossed the hissing water on them. Come winter, they took them apart and piled the sections on the bank to assemble again in the late spring. Those times bred tough men to supply the prospectors who made scars on the slopes of the Bonanza Hills.

My attention was drawn to magpies making their harsh calls from the willow brush. Now and then I saw the black and white splashes of their wings against the foliage. That kind of activity needed to be checked out, so I strolled over there.

The magpies scattered and perched in the spruces. On the moss was what was left of a caribou. A hunter had made a kill here a few days ago. All that remained was a badly torn stomach, some legs, and part of the head. Something besides the magpies had been feasting here.

I examined the area for signs. There was a movement along the slope. I trained the glasses and saw an animal about the size of a fox but darker and chunkier. A wolverine, then another, and finally a third. They loped across a clearing, headed my way, and into a thick brush patch.

Suddenly a flock of ptarmigan cackled and flurried into the air, their white wings quickly setting in downward curves as they sailed along the slope and tipped to a landing. Two wolverines reared from the brush the way bird dogs do to get a better look over heavy cover. They cut back and forth, working like beagles. One stood up and looked at me, ducked, then returned to stare again. The others were on his flanks. They were small wolverines, perhaps a little more than half grown. I wondered where the mother was. They shrank into the brush and I didn't see them again.

It was time to head for home. I would remember the sounds of the Chilikadrotna, savage, awesome, terrifyingly beautiful as it smashed white against the boulders and seethed angrily toward the sea.

A stroke of good luck came on the return trip. The wind was at my back as I kneeled on the canoe bottom and rode the big swells.

The current in the connecting stream was too strong to paddle against. I unwound a nylon line and hitched one end to the stern ring and the other end to the thwart just behind the bow seat. I picked up the middle of the line, let the canoe ride back with the current and walked along the bank. The canoe rode high against the flow and was easy to control as I towed it to the upper lake.

After the long paddle the cabin's gleam on the beach was a comfort. The more I see it the more I love it. Surely there is no stretch on the lakeshore as sheltered as mine.

After a supper of navy beans, I sat on my threshold and gazed off toward the volcanic mountains. I had been close to them today. The Chilikadrotna River showed me the beautiful fish and I returned them to her. I thought of the sights I had seen. The price was physical toll. Money does little good back here. It could not buy the fit feeling that surged through my arms and shoulders. It could not buy the feeling of accomplishment. I had been my own tour guide, and my own power had been my transportation. This great big country was my playground, and I could afford the price it demanded.

– Reflections –

I sat on the spruce chunk listening to Hope Creek rushing down the cut just beyond the willows. This was one of the good places to sit and watch the action along the Cowgill Benches.

I was proud of my cabin, my woodshed, and my cache. The actual cash layout had been just a shade over forty dollars, and that figure included the glass window Babe had flown in but which was still in storage. The Mylar thermopane had been better for my needs.

Needs? I guess that is what bothers so many folks. They keep expanding their needs until they are dependent on too many things and too many other people. I don't understand economics, and I suppose the country would be in a real mess if people suddenly cut out a lot of things they don't need. I wonder how many things in the average American home could be eliminated if the question were asked, "Must I really have this?" I guess most of the extras are chalked up to comfort or saving time.

Funny thing about comfort—one man's comfort is another man's misery. Most people don't work hard enough physically anymore, and comfort is not easy to find. It is surprising how comfortable a hard bunk can be after you come down off a mountain.

I've seen grown men pick at food. They can't be hungry in the first place.

Or maybe their food has been too fancy and with all the choices they've had, they don't really know what they enjoy anymore.

What a man never has, he never misses. I learned something from the big game animals. Their food is pretty much the same from day to day. I don't vary my fare too much either, and I've never felt better in my life. I don't confuse my digestive system, I just season simple food with hunger. Food is fuel, and the best fuel I have found is oatmeal and all the stuff you can mix with it, like raisins and honey and brown sugar; meat and gravy and sourdough biscuits to sop up the juices with; a kettle of beans you can dip into every day; rice or spuds with fish, and some fresh greens now and then.

I enjoy working for my heat. I don't just press a button or twist a thermostat dial. I use the big crosscut saw and the axe, and while I'm getting my heat supply I'm working up an appetite that makes simple food just as appealing as anything a French chef could create. I've never found anything I like better to drink than Hope Creek water. The good feeling I get out of lungfuls of mountain air and draughts of sweet water from the snows is probably as good as any "high" I would get out of a bottle or a pill. But of course not many have a chance to live in unspoiled country.

I have learned patience, learned to take my time and try to do a job right by first figuring it out. No sense to rushing and going off half cocked; there's plenty of time out here. No sense complaining if the weather turns sour—make your job fit the day. Grandmother Nature is in control, and you better just wait until she sees fit to give you the weather that is right for another job you have to do.

Distance is relative. You learn that in time. A trip for me down to the lower end of the lower lake takes three hours by canoe if I don't have the wind to fight. That's a distance of about eight and a half miles. With a motor on the canoe I could make the trip in under an hour, but a motor's noise stills the sounds of the wilderness.

Eight and a half miles can be covered in minutes with a car on an expressway, but what does a man see? What he gains in time he loses in benefit to his body and his mind. At my pace I can notice things. A bubble on the water, an arctic tern's breast tinged with the blue reflection of the lake. The landscape is not just a monotonous blur on either side. The stroke of a paddle moves you forward about eleven feet. Sometimes I get lost in the rhythm of the paddling. I even count the strokes it takes to get me to a point of land. The play of muscles in one's arms and shoulders, and the feel of palm against worn wood, are preferable to glancing at a speedometer.

I have surprised myself with what I could make with simple tools when a definite need arose. I made a tap out of a nail and cut a thread for a homemade screw that my tripod needed. I made a spring for the automatic timer on the camera, and countless other times repaired the camera, the gas lantern, and other accessories. I made a crimping tool to scallop the edges of some tin trays I fashioned from gas cans. I have made all kinds of things from gas cans. I don't think a man knows what he actually can do until he is challenged.

Nature provides so many things if one has the eye to notice them. It is a pleasure to see what you can use instead of buying it all packaged and ready-made. Several stumps with just the right flare gave me my wooden hinges. Burls and peculiar branch growths afforded me bowls and wooden spoons and clothes hangers. Driftwood provided me with a curtain rod and my spruce buck horns. I found spruce cones to be as effective as Brillo pads or steel wool to scour my pots. Stones of all colors and shapes were the raw material for my fireplace. When I did resort to manufactured products such as polyethylene, nails, and cement, I felt as though I had cheated. I was not being true to the philosophy I was trying to follow.

I do think a man has missed a very deep feeling of satisfaction if he has never created or at least completed something with his own two hands. We have grown accustomed to work on pieces of things instead of wholes. It is a way of life with us now. The emphasis is on teamwork. I believe this trend bears much of the blame for the loss of pride in one's work, the kind of pride the old craftsman felt when he started a job and finished it and stood back and admired it. How does a man on an assembly line feel any pride in the final product that rolls out at the other end?

I realize that men working together can perform miracles such as sending men to walk on the surface of the moon. There is definitely a need and a place for teamwork, but there is also a need for an individual sometime in his life to forget the world of parts and pieces and put something together on his own— complete something. He's got to create.

Man is dependent upon man. I would be the last to argue that point. Babe brought me things that other men made or produced. We need each other; but nevertheless, in a jam the best friend you have is yourself.

I have often thought about what I would do out here if I were stricken with a serious illness, if I broke a leg, cut myself badly, or had an attack of appendicitis. Almost as quickly as the thought came, I dismissed it. Why worry about something that isn't? Worrying about something that might happen is not a healthy pastime. A man's a fool to live his life under a shadow like that. Maybe that's how an ulcer begins.

I have thought briefly about getting caught in rock slides or falling from a rock face. If that happened, I would probably perish on the mountain in much the same way many of the big animals do. I would be long gone before anyone found me. My only wish would be that folks wouldn't spend a lot of time searching. When the time comes for a man to look his Maker in the eye, where better could the meeting be held than in the wilderness?

News never changes much. It's just the same things happening to different people. I would rather experience things happening to me than read about them happening to others. I am my own newspaper and my own radio. I honestly don't believe that man was meant to know everything going on in the world, all at the same time. A man turns on the TV and all those commentators bombard him with the local, the national and the international news. The newspapers do the same thing, and the poor guy with all the immediate problems of his own life is burdened with those of the whole world.

I don't know what the answer is. In time man gets used to almost anything, but the problem seems to be that technology is advancing faster than he can adjust to it. I think it's time we started applying the brakes, slowing down our greed and slowing down the world.

I have found that some of the simplest things have given me the most pleasure. They didn't cost me a lot of money either. They just worked on my senses. Did you ever pick very large blueberries after a summer rain? Walk through a grove of cottonwoods, open like a park, and see the blue sky beyond the shimmering gold of the leaves? Pull on dry woolen socks after you've peeled off the wet ones? Come in out of the subzero and shiver yourself warm in front of a wood fire? The world is full of such things.

I've watched many hunters come and go. I don't begrudge a hunter his Dall ram if he climbs to the crags to get one and packs it down the mountain. If he does this, he has earned those curved horns to put up on his wall. Yet there are so many who have not earned what they proudly exhibit. Even though the hunt may have cost them thousands of dollars, they did not pay the full price for it.

I have no doubt that to others I am an oddball in many ways. The Lord waited a little too long to put me on one of his worlds. I don't like the look of progress, if that is what it's called. I would have liked the beginnings better. That's why this place has taken hold of me. It's still in those early stages and man hasn't left too many marks on the land. Surely I have been places up and down these mountains where other men have never been. How long before all this will change as the other places have changed?

I've seen a lot of sights from this old spruce chunk, and have thought a lot of thoughts. The more I think about it, the better off I think I am. The crime rate up here is close to zero. I forget what it is like to be sick or have a cold. I don't have bills coming in every month to pay for things I really don't need. My legs and canoe provide my transportation. They take me as far as I care to go.

To see game you must move a little and look a lot. What first appears to be a branch turns into that big caribou bull up there on the benches—I wonder what he thinks about? Is his brain just a blank as he lies there blinking in the sun and chewing his cud? I wonder if he feels as I do, that this small part of the world is enough to think about?

– *Until Another Spring* –

■ *September 21st.* Forty-eight degrees. A gusty breeze down the lake that made the whitecaps toss.

I told Babe on his last trip that I would go out on September twenty-fifth or the first good day after that. I intended to spend the winter Outside. Dad was not his active self and he could use another pair of hands.

Babe allowed it was a good idea. "You'll appreciate the wilderness more," he said, "when you see that sick country again."

The first day of fall and halfway to the shortest day of the year. It hardly seems possible. There is a batch of chores to do. Get the canoe ready to go into storage, wash and dry the heavy clothes that will stay behind.

There is always a sadness about packing. I guess you wonder if where you're going is as good as where you've been.

I watched the sun go down, and watched the flames it left on the clouds. In less than a week the sun will sink behind the pyramid mountain. I remembered when it disappeared behind that same peak on its journey to the longest day.

■ *September 22nd.* Frost on the beach. Clear, calm, and thirty degrees.

Today would be cleanup day. My first stop was Glacier Creek, where I buried some civilization scraps left behind by sheep hunters. Most hunters have poor housekeeping habits. Their wives must spoil them at home. Out here there is no one to pick up after them.

Next stop the upper end. Much garbage to hide there as well, ration boxes, tin cans, and plastic wrappers.

After being deserted for a couple of years, the beaver lodge has a lived-in look. I see a big supply of willow groceries anchored nearby. The dam has been repaired. There are drag trails leading out in all directions. Good to see the beaver back on the upper end.

Back at the cabin by late afternoon. Seven spruce grouse picking in the gravel of my path. If they would eat rolled oats, I would have a nice flock of wild chickens. Are they becoming friendlier now that it is almost time to leave?

After supper I busied myself oiling tools and getting them ready to store.

The surf was restless on the gravel of the beach.

■ *September 23rd.* Twenty-five degrees and fog patches.

This morning I watched a bull moose and a cow across the lake. The cow was above him. The bull climbed, and the cow acted afraid and tried to get by him down the mountain. Back and forth across the slope they trotted. The old boy worked like a cutting horse to block her every turn. Finally she broke through and headed down country. He had to be content to follow below. I lost them in the brush. Later on I heard a bawling repeated several times, and spotted a bull moose at the edge of the timber. Then a cow, another bull, and a second cow. Moose all over the place. The rutting season is at hand.

I cleaned up the sheep hunters' camps at the lower end of the lake and the connecting stream. They, too, had moved in for a spell and left their stains on the land.

The red salmon run is over. I see no more finners along the shore. I saw some dead ones floating today and a good many other carcasses along the beaches. The sanitation department will have to get busy.

The caribou hindquarter, which had been hanging under the cache for over five weeks, was hard and dry on the outside but moist and red inside. I cut some for the birds, and sliced off a steak for supper.

■ *September 24th.* Clear, calm, and forty-five degrees. September never saw a finer morning.

Today I will store many things away, close up the remaining window and put the pole props under the purlin logs. I wish I was opening up instead of closing.

Amazing what a man accumulates! I rearranged my cache and now it is filled to bulging. I hope Babe is right, that few are brave enough to climb that high. I will store the big ladder in the timber and put the cache ladder in Spike's cabin.

I saw the sunlight sparkle on the wet paddle blade for the last time as I rode the canoe down to its storage place in Spike's cabin. All these preparations point toward winter, but the fine weather doesn't believe it.

I would leave a few last-minute things.

Tomorrow I would be ready, just in case.

■ *September 25th.* Clear, calm, and thirty-two degrees.

Just finished the breakfast dishes when I heard the plane. Babe drifted into the beach with a grin on his face.

"It's the twenty-fifth," he said. "I've been watching the weather. It won't last. Figured I'd better come and get you while it was fair."

There was no hurry, but Babe packed things to the plane while I put the covers over the windows, secured the stovepipe, and carried in a fresh supply of wood. The birds got many odds and ends from the kitchen and worked in desperation to pack it away in the timber.

Babe watched them. "They're going to miss welfare," he said.

Time to go. The birds were perched silently in the spruces. A last check on the woodshed. The weasel whisked into the woodpile, switched ends, and peered out at me. I could hear the squirrel singing from a cluster of spruce cones. At last he was getting rid of me.

I closed my door and turned the locking lever for the last time.

Full throttle down the calm lake and up on the step. One last look at the beautiful country I knew so well. The brave gleam of my cabin logs and cache. There was a lot of me down there. Sixteen months, but such days are a bonus that don't count in your life span at all.

That night during a gathering at Babe's place, I felt a civilized cold germ taking hold.

– Epilogue –

On Dick's cabin table was left a message:

> This cabin has been my home for the past sixteen months, and it is with regret
> that I leave it for a time. I think it would be safe to say that I have hiked thousands
> of miles in my total of two years at Twin Lakes. In the past sixteen months alone
> I have exposed more than 3,000 feet of 8mm movie film and many rolls of 35mm
> film on the wildlife and the scenery of the area, plus the building of my cabin,
> woodshed, and cache.
>
> In my travels I have picked up and disposed of much litter left by others.
> Many fail to show respect that the area deserves.
>
> You didn't find a padlock on my door (maybe I should have put one on) for
> I feel that a cabin in the wilderness should be open to those who need shelter.
> My charge for the use of it is reasonable, I think, although some no doubt will be
> unable to afford what I ask, and that is—take care of it as if you had carved it out
> with hand tools as I did. If when you leave your conscience is clear, then you have
> paid the full amount.
>
> This is beautiful country. It is even more beautiful when the animals are left alive.
> Thank you for your cooperation.

R.L. Proenneke

– *Afterword* –

Dick Proenneke celebrated the 30th anniversary of his cabin-building at Twin Lakes on May 30, 1998. Since the original publication of *One Man's Wilderness* in the spring of 1973, he has been on the scene, except for several trips to the Lower 48. Currently in his eighties, he chooses not to stay the winters; chores once routine require more effort these days.

What has he been doing all this time? He has served as the ultimate guardian of the Twins. He has tried to make pristine again what others have soiled. Removing campsite blemishes and cleansing the littered beaches from his Eden have long been an obsession. During these rounds, his cameras have always been ready to shoot dramatic encounters—the nest of a fiercely aggressive goshawk, a wild-eyed, huge-racked caribou bull swimming to out-distance his paddle thrusts, the rescue of a bawling moose calf from a marauding bear. He has located bear dens and even crawled into them after they were vacant to find a surprisingly sweet odor instead of a stench. He has discovered wolf dens, usually near the water. He has explored glaciers and the surrounding crags, wearing out much footgear in countless miles over challenging terrain. He continues to thrill to the haunting choruses of wolves, especially beneath flickering veils of the northern lights.

An event he will never forget happened in the spring of 1976 when he flew a Piper J3 Cub up from Iowa. He and his brother Raymond had serviced this plane and brought it to perfection. All that summer he kept it moored between occasional flights in the bight opposite his cabin. Enroute home in the fall, it almost killed him. He had been following the Alaskan Highway. At Sheep Mountain Pass his carburetor iced up. The motor quit. A forced landing was imminent. With a deadening jolt, he plowed into an up-slope. When he regained consciousness, he could barely move. No one would find him where he was. Somehow he painfully bellied his way up to the highway edge. A couple in a passing pickup truck stopped to help him. They drove him to Gulkana, where he received emergency treatment. From there, he was transferred to Anchorage and hospitalized for serious back trauma. It proved to be a lengthy, frustrating experience, but he returned in the spring to his cabin.

That ordeal over, he focused on his cameras. Over the years he has exposed many rolls of 35mm film, as well as reels of 8mm and 16mm. The National Park Service produced *One Man's Alaska*, featuring his striking photography. This promotional film is available from Alaska National History Association in Anchorage or National Park Service at Lake Clark. A videotape followed, *The Frozen North*, from Bob Swerer Productions at Fort Collins, Colorado. Dick's fine cinematography is presented, and he does much of the narration.

During Dick's long tenure, Twin Lakes became part of Lake Clark National Park and Preserve. Today, a ranger station is situated near the foot of the lower lake. Dick has had contact with it by "walkie-talkie." Travelers, many from other countries, have flown in for float trips down the Chilikadrotna River, which begins there. The cabin's guest register lists hundreds of visitors, including former governor of Alaska Jay Hammond and the late singer John Denver, who have come over the years to meet and talk with Dick.

This year, Dick formally entrusted his homestead to the Park Service. His cabin will be maintained as a historic site. He may return to stay in it anytime he wishes. And while he may not make the trip physically again, his spirit will always linger in the perfect notches of his logs.

Sam Keith
Anderson, South Carolina
September 28, 1998

– *About the Author* –

Alaska was always on Sam Keith's mind. Ever since Keith was a child, his father, a wildlife artist and naturalist, had instilled in him the dream of going there. During the Depression, Keith was a member of the Civilian Conservation Corps in Northeastern Oregon. In World War II he served in the Pacific as a combat air crewman in the first Marine "Billy Mitchell" bombing squadron, "The Flying Nightmares."

After being discharged, he attended Cornell University where he majored in English and elected wildlife courses. Keith then moved to Alaska where he immersed himself in "The Great Land"—Kodiak Island, the Alaska peninsula, and the Kenai. After more than three years, he returned to New England, where he "camped" behind a typewriter, and pursued a career as a writer.

Writing did not come easy for Keith, and he felt stalled at a crossroads until he married Jane. She gave him not only a lovely daughter, Laurel, but also the direction to enter a teaching career, which lasted 26 years. At one point he fortuitously seized the opportunity to spend two weeks with Dick Proenneke, his former Alaskan partner, to see a cabin, a cache, and untamed country. *One Man's Wilderness* was launched.